What Did You Say?
Memories on a road less travelled

by D. Hugh Gillard

(a.k.a Douglas Gillard)
(a.k.a. Nudnass Niller)

4th Floor Press, Inc.
www.4thfloorpress.com

Library and Archives Canada Cataloguing in Publication

Gillard, D. Hugh, 1948-, author

What did you say? : memories on a road less travelled / by

D. Hugh Gillard (a.k.a Douglas Gillard).

Issued in print and electronic formats.

ISBN 978-1-897530-43-6 (pbk.).ISBN 978-1-897530-44-3 (mobi)

1. Gillard, D. Hugh, 1948-. 2. Cleft palate--Patients--Canada--
Biography. 3. People with disabilities--Canada--Biography. 4.
Petroleum industry and trade--Canada--Employees--Biography. 5.
Businessmen--Canada--Biography. I. Title.

RD525.G54 2013   362.19'75225092   C2013-905202-X

C2013-905203-8

Published by 4th Floor Press, Inc.

www.4thfloorpress.com

1st Printing 2013

2nd Printing 2013

3rd Printing 2014

Printed in Canada

The author can be contacted at hughgillard@shaw.ca

www.hughgillard.com

DEDICATION

To all the children who are afflicted with a cleft lip and or palate. May their lives be as fulfilled as mine has been. And to all my family and friends and career associates, past and present, who looked beyond the surface and accepted me for who I really was.

ACKNOWLEDGEMENTS

I wish to thank my wife Rosemary who helped edit the first draft of What Did You Say?, making it at least presentable to a professional publisher. I also wish to thank the staff at 4th Floor Press, Inc. and in particular Wendy Lukasiewicz, my marvelous book editor, Anne Bougie-Johnson for her guidance and endless patience throughout the publishing process, and Johanna Bates, for her strong encouragement.

I am also grateful to Bruna Martinuzzi who encouraged me to put pen to paper. "The world needs your story," she insisted.

TABLE OF CONTENTS

Two roads diverged in a wood, and I—
I took the one less traveled by,
and that has made all the difference.

Robert Frost,

The Road Not Taken
American poet (1874 - 1963)

INTRODUCTION

I couldn't remember when I had been so excited. Maybe it was when I first rode my bike more than ten feet without falling off, or maybe it was the first time I wasn't picked dead last for the noon-hour ballgame. The next morning would be a big step towards life on my own: my first interview for my first permanent job. I had even bought my first suit and tie, which I would hopefully wear at my first job.

In 1972, jobs were available for new Business graduates, but the competition for the best jobs was still very intense. Various companies would come to campus and interview prospective candidates from the pool of upcoming graduates. This was the pre-fax, pre-wireless, pre-Internet age, so students most often found out about potential job opportunities through notices posted on the bulletin board near the Dean's office.

Texaco Canada, a large multinational oil company, had posted a notice for an entry-level marketing position that particularly caught my attention. "Applicants must possess a degree in Marketing. Oil and gas work experience an asset." From all the applications, Texaco would select a maximum of three candidates from four different universities across Canada for interviews. The University of Calgary was one of them.

I would soon be graduating with a Bachelor of Commerce

degree majoring in Marketing. I had excellent marks as well as experience in the oil and gas sector from working the previous three summers in the oilfields. On paper, I was the perfect fit: the right degree, the right marks, the right experience. Clearly this was *the* job for me. With high hopes, I mailed my resume to Texaco's head office in Toronto.

Not long after, an envelope arrived with the Texaco logo boldly stamped on the upper left corner. My heart raced as I opened it. It was like an Academy Award moment before the announcement of the winner. Good news. I had been selected as one of three candidates at the University of Calgary, and one of twelve students across Canada, to be interviewed at a predetermined future date and time. "Yes!" I said, pumping my fist.

My "moment of opportunity" could not come quickly enough. Like a potential first-round draft pick, I nervously headed to the Texaco interview. The walk from the parking lot to the university's Social Science Building—the same walk I had taken countless times over the previous four years— seemed shorter than usual. Only this time I thought about how far I had come from my setbacks in elementary school some twenty years earlier. I felt confident, but not cocky.

Upon finding and then nervously entering the interview room, I observed two older gentlemen (anyone over forty looked seriously old back then) sitting behind a table. Both stood up, shook my hand, and introduced themselves.

"Hello, I'm Douglas Gillard. Pleased to meet you," I said

and took a seat.

After a few seconds of pause, the older of the two said, "What did you say?"

"Douglas Gillard," I said again.

"So, we understand you're interested in the marketing position."

"Yes."

There was another pause, but this time it seemed like hours. The two gentlemen exchanged eye contact with each other like some kind of secret signal.

"Well, I'm sorry, but this interview is over."

Thinking I had heard incorrectly, I asked, "What was that?"

"The interview is over."

"Are you serious?"

"Yes."

"Why?"

"There's no way you can be a marketer with the way you talk. People won't understand you and you need to be able to communicate."

And, with that, the shortest interview on record was over. It lasted no more than ninety seconds from beginning to end, including introductions. It had taken me longer to put on my necktie. Without a single question, they decided that I was not qualified. Nothing too complicated or thought provoking. If you talked differently, you simply didn't qualify. I was DQ'd before my first game.

It was shock and awe thirty years before Iraq. I walked out of the interview room, not really believing what had just happened. I could hardly breathe and could barely hold back the tears. The walk back to my car was the polar opposite of the walk onto campus. My confidence and high expectations were gone, replaced with emptiness. The walk back seemed to take forever.

Everything I had worked for, all the progress I had made, all the optimism I had built up, had evaporated in a matter of seconds. It was my very own personal Armageddon. This experience would revisit me for years to come and be the milestone against which I would measure my career progress.

CHAPTER 1
A Rough Start

Everyone has a different first memory. Even though I can recall standing in the crib at my grandparents' house and looking up at them, I'm pretty sure my first real memory was when I was four or five. I had just said something to my mom and she turned to my younger sister, Jean, and asked, "What did he say?" Jean repeated, word for word, what I had just said. When I think back on this, I am amazed. Jean and I played together constantly and at three years old she already knew me best. She was the only one who understood me and was my best friend. This incident has remained locked in my memory as a watershed moment: the moment I realized something was different about me. Exactly how different I had no idea.

Rodney "No Respect" Dangerfield once quipped, "When I was born, the doctor slapped my mother!" I'm sure the country doctor who delivered me didn't slap my mother, but my face was one that only a mother could love. And, at first glance, I doubt if she did. I can't imagine the shocked look on the faces of the two new parents when Dr. O'Brien told them the news: "Your baby has a harelip and cleft palate." Who would have blamed them if they had asked, "Why us?" or "What did we do wrong?" Every parent hopes for a healthy baby and then for a boy or girl, in that order, and my parents were no different. Surely they cried, but as disappointed as they were, they must also have been at a loss as to what to do next.

Parent counselling was unheard of back then, so my parents were on their own. As Mom once said to a nephew whose girlfriend had just had an unplanned baby, "You can't send it back now." It was her way of saying that one has to accept what happened and deal with the outcome. Mom and Dad stared reality in the face, accepted what happened, and simply got on with dealing with it.

Despite extensive medical research, the cause of the cleft physical defect is still unknown. Recent theories focus on a lack of folic acid in the mother's diet during pregnancy. Even if that's the case, I'm quite sure nobody living on the Canadian prairies in the late 1940s knew what folic acid was, much less knew what to do about it.

"Cleft lip and palate" is the modern term for the affliction. The term "harelip" referred to the physical similarities between the cleft lip and a rabbit's, or hare's, lip. Fortunately, the medical official in charge of naming diseases and afflictions had the decency to recognize that an affliction named after an animal was not exactly endearing and, in fact, was downright degrading. "Cleft" has now become the common description, but I suspect that harelip is still used extensively, particularly in jokes, though not around me. These days, most people's sensitivities have grown more acute.

The cleft deformity occurs in about 1.4 out of every 1,000 Caucasian American newborns. Research the causes on the Internet and you'll find a range of explanations from genetics to environment. Genetically, there are no less than eleven different syndrome possibilities. Now, in the 1940s, the prairies didn't have any nuclear power plants and had zero pollution, so I think genetics were a more likely cause. However, three people had the same deformity as mine on that sparse prairie where I grew up. There weren't even a thousand people within fifty miles, so maybe it was something in the water after all.

If you drew the lucky *long* straw, you got the unilateral (single) cleft lip and no cleft palate. If you drew the unlucky *short* straw, you got the bilateral (both sides) cleft lip and cleft palate. The straw I drew was in between: single cleft lip and a cleft palate. My first reconstructive surgery occurred six weeks after birth. With a one-inch wide gash in my lip, gums, and roof of my mouth, how I was fed is a mystery to me. Asking one's mother how you were breastfed is not exactly dinner table conversation. Suffice to say, a solution was found, as I now weigh around two hundred pounds.

The nearest hospital to perform such reconstructive surgery was the University Hospital in Edmonton, nearly two hundred miles away. With a lady friend along in the car to help hold me the entire trip, Mom and Dad drove to the hospital for my first of many surgeries. The plastic surgeon was Dr. William Hitchen, one of the top surgeons in Canada. Rumour had it that he had a drinking problem, but fortunately he was either sober that day or there was some divine assistance in the operating room. By all accounts, he did a good job putting back together what all the King's men could not.

Two and a half years later, I was back on the operating table for follow-up surgery. My last until I was fifteen. The most obvious evidence of these surgeries was a severe scar that ran straight up from my top lip to my left nostril. That side of my nose was clearly smaller than the right side. The top gums that had the "cleft" or "break" right through it on the left side were now repaired, although not straight. All of this was set on a flat face profile, sort of like the ancient paintings before artists figured out depth perception.

You might ask where the teeth came in with such a large gap. Good question and I don't have the answer. What I do know is my eyetooth came down from the roof of my mouth, just inside the gums. It never bothered me and is still there today, totally invisible, but dental hygienists (a new one every visit, it seems) always express shock. "What's that doing up there?" they'll ask, or "You have quite a jigsaw puzzle in there!" I was always embarrassed about my crooked teeth and rarely smiled in pictures until they were straightened in my twenties.

My top front teeth came in so crooked that the simple act of eating corn on the cob took longer than cooking it. Rather than resembling the rounded roof of a grand cathedral, the roof of my mouth resembled an unfinished vaulted ceiling. That ceiling also had a built-in air vent: a tiny hole existed from the top of my mouth up to the inside of my nose. A hole in the roof of one's mouth presents some practical limitations, including not being able to blow up a balloon. As a kid I would try to pinch my nose with one hand while trying to hold the balloon with the other hand and blow into it. At birthday parties, the kids thought I was the entertainment. Whenever I leaned over and drank from a water fountain, water would pour out of my nose.

Despite having enough room for water to come out the wrong way, my upper nostrils were still pinched off enough that I mouth breathed almost all the time. This caused another issue. My bottom lip would hang down, as though I had a total lack of muscle control. Perfect for saxophone playing, but not exactly child star material.

My nose was acceptable if you didn't mind one nostril being smaller than the other. Later in life, the shape was the least of my worries. Maybe it was all the surgeries or maybe simply rosacea, but it grew redder as I grew older. The red nose often led to absurd conversations on elevators: "How was the skiing? Your nose is really sunburned!" After the umpteenth time of such questions, I soon learned the easy answer: "Snow conditions were great." I don't even ski. Strangers think I'm an alcoholic. My close friend Ozzie once teased me at a barbeque by asking if I'd mind sticking my nose on the briquettes to ignite them. Now that humour I love. Life is too short if you can't laugh at yourself.

Another "dot" in my "connect-the-dots" syndrome is hearing loss. It was detected later in my life, but not before significantly contributing to my struggles trying to hear the teachers in school.

And that was about it, except for one more detail: speech!

Speech was my biggest adversary. My voice came out irritatingly nasal with little or no inflections. Everyone always thought I had a cold. Even sixty years later, I'm often asked, "What nationality are you? You're Canadian? I would never have guessed."

Words starting or ending with *s, se, sc, ce, n, d, g, l, es, eg, as, tr, v,* and *z* were very challenging. The rest were just challenging. Every word was a struggle. Numbers like six, sixteen, thirty, or any combination thereof, were non-starters. Saying my brother Stuart's name came out sounding like "Sterd" and later "Stert." Scott came out "Stot," or worse, "Snot," and it still does! It didn't matter how a word ended because I couldn't pronounce the ending anyway. The *d*s and the *t*s at the end were always silent. "An" and "and" came out identically, as did hundreds of other words, like "happen" and "happened." Any two words that started or ended remotely the same came out of my mouth the same. I had my very own book of homonyms: "rice" and "rights," "eggs" and "eights," "dog" and "nod." The list was endless.

I could not even say my own name, Douglas Gillard. At

best, it came out "Nudnass Niller," and that's being generous. Not being able to say one's name when you're a child is the ultimate humiliation. Too bad I hadn't been born in the Deep South and named Billy Bob. Or better yet, Tom, Dick, or Harry. The fewer letters in a name, the better. Single syllable words are best, providing they contain the right letters. I don't blame my parents for their name choice. In their minds, Douglas was a fine Scottish name and Gillard was not optional. They had no way of knowing that had I been named Tom, after my grandfather, life would have been much easier.

Something else compounded my speech impediment: enunciation laziness. I rarely finish a word, even to this day. I believe much of the problem stems from being hard of hearing. I often don't hear the inflections of words, especially the endings. As a young kid, I remember singing the Johnny Cash tune "Give My Love to Rose," about a dying man just out of prison and trying to get back home. My brother, Stuart, overheard me and yelled from another room, "They let me out of *Frisco* not out of *Crystal*!"

Often, the person I was speaking to would usually guess what they thought I was saying. If the first wild guess was right, we would move on. If not, I'd try again, following the natural human tendency to speak louder if someone doesn't understand you. For added emphasis, I would use more lip and tongue action than Pavarotti warming up for the opera. At the forty-decibel point, I usually had to change tactics and use another word that they might understand. If they were wrong again, I would simply nod as though they had finally understood me. I should go into partnership with Rosetta Stone—there's an untapped translation market out there!

A line from the classic movie *Cool Hand Luke* perfectly describes a typical breakfast order: "What we have here . . . is . . . a failure to communicate."

"What would you like, honey?"

"I'll have srammle aids, please."

"What did you say?

"Uh, aids."

"Sorry, honey, I didn't hear you."

"AIDS!" I would point to the picture of two fried eggs on the menu.

"Oh, eggs! That's what you want. And is that all?"

"Yes." I gave up ordering the eggs scrambled. If the picture had ham in it instead of bacon, then ham it would be.

"Thank you, honey, coming right up."

I like restaurants that have menus with pictures.

CHAPTER 2
A Little History

Although Canada had been an independent nation since 1867, the British still dominated all aspects of Canadian business and politics for decades afterwards. The British tendency to do things orderly and properly permeated all things, including at least one brilliant decision taken in the late 1800s. The Canadian Government decided to survey the entire prairie territories that stretched thousands of square miles, comprising millions of acres of raw land. All of this took place long before the railroad, or roads, for that matter. All future development, including farming, would transact on the basis of these surveys. There would be no "every man for himself," Oklahoma-type land rush on the prairies. The Canadian way would be orderly! One mile by one mile comprised a section of 640 acres, with thirty-six sections to a township. Each section was subdivided into quarter sections, all marked at each corner with iron pegs pounded into the ground with its surveyed location etched in.

The Government, along with the Canadian Pacific Railway Company (CPR), which by now stretched in a single line across Canada, was encouraging settlers to head west and settle the land. If you could successfully farm a quarter section of land, you then had the right to buy a second adjoining quarter.

The CPR promoted the concept, often with the propaganda of glossy artwork of the Promised Land pasted all over eastern Canada and Europe. They were betting that the future farmers would have grain and livestock to ship back to market on their rails. Monopolies were legal and very profitable.

If my grandfather had had a GPS when he struck out to homestead, it may well have told him to "Take the northbound train from Calgary approximately one hundred miles to Lacombe; take the eastbound train approximately forty miles to Stettler; head east by foot, horseback, or oxen-pulled wagon about seventy-five miles; make a right hand turn and head south about five miles." All the while saying, "Recalculating."

There was no GPS in 1907 when Thomas Gillard and his two brothers decided to immigrate to Canada and homestead. Thomas had bought his way out of the British Royal Navy, having served on the ship *Formidable.* When he first arrived in Canada, he worked at a stone quarry near Cochrane, Alberta, before deciding to try homesteading.

The northwest quarter of Section 20, Township 35, Range 9, West of the 4th Meridian, ultimately became the ranch. His brother Arthur settled on the northeast quarter of the same section, and brother Bryce settled four miles due south. By oxen or horse, they hauled their belongings, equipment, and building materials from Stettler to the homestead. After locating the quarter sections they had chosen earlier, sight unseen, and with only the help of a rough map and inscribed steel pegs, they built a sod house and started farming from nothing. If they could get the land to crop stage, they would have the right to buy the adjoining quarters, which they did.

The Gillard farm turned out to be two miles southeast of Throne (established after the railroad came in 1911) in the heart of central Alberta, on an absolutely flat piece of land. Except for the odd bunch of scrub poplar trees, the only things higher than the trees were two distinct hills, the Nose and the Neutral Hills, on the far horizon some fifteen miles away. (An 1888 map of the territories showed these hills to be in Saskatchewan territory. In 1905, when Alberta and Saskatchewan became provinces, the border was "drawn" farther east, leaving the hills within Alberta.)

The early 1900s are relatively modern times, but vast herds of buffalo had roamed those lands only thirty years before. Around the same time, 5,000 Indians, mostly Assiniboine, Blackfoot, Crow, and Cree, signed Treaty Number 6 at Sounding Lake, to the northeast. The first white man had settled in what would be the Coronation region only forty years earlier ("Shadows of the Neutrals," Anne Speight, the *Saskatchewan Herald* (Battleford), August 26, 1878).

As far as the eye could see, this vast prairie land was covered with grass known as Prairie Wool, a high quality grass ideal for livestock. However, when John Palliser explored the land in 1857 for the British Government, he noted, "this area would never be fit for settlement as it was too dry for raising crops" ("Shadows of the Neutrals," Anne Speight). His observation was accurate, for as good as the soil was for livestock, the region was semi-arid and had limited topsoil and rain, making it less than ideal for growing grain. My grandparents were to find this out the hard way.

Tom (Pop) and Arthur Gillard each built a house with about a quarter mile separating the two. For efficiency sake, they must have concluded it would be best if they acted as a partnership and built one massive three-story hip roof barn to house the livestock and feed. They chose Tom's place for the barn that, when completed, was visible for miles around. But, partnerships have a habit of not surviving, for every imaginable reason, from greed to spousal relationships. The Gillard brothers were no exception. The one thing they had built in common became the subject of a major decision when the partnership collapsed. Each brother already had his own house, but what to do with the barn? Who got the barn? In their minds, the solution was simple: saw the barn in half. They had homesteaded together at considerable risk and sacrifice, they had started their families together, they had built the farm with their own hands, and now with these same hands they were about to literally saw their partnership in half. The rural tradition of "barn raising" had run amuck. Instead of all the neighbours raising the barn, they all gathered at the Gillard farm to tear the barn in half.

It must have been a most unique sight that spring morning when the severing of both the partnership and the barn began in earnest. No doubt the sight and squeak of the handsaws cutting the wood would be talked about for years. I have often wondered how they both felt that morning of the beginning of the end. *Choosing* the halfway spot to start the first cut would be the easy part; *making* the first cut would be excruciating. Did they not wonder why it had come to this? Was it too late to change their minds?

Like some self-imposed vow of silence, the reason for the breakup was never discussed or passed down to future generations. I recently asked my Great-uncle Arthur's son, Claude, now over ninety years old, if he knew anything about the breakup. He didn't know for sure, but assumed his dad had simply wanted his own barn. However, I vaguely recall as a young boy overhearing that the spouses did not get along. Tom and Arthur had to choose between the barn and their wives—a dilemma to be sure.

Tom would keep the north half of the barn where it stood and Great-uncle Arthur would take the south half to a location close to his house, a quarter mile away. There is no record of how long it took, but one can guess given the immensity of the job. Cutting the massive barn in half was the easy part. It would take a lot of work to raise the south half high enough to put wheels underneath and then move it by oxen. Perhaps they cut it down into separate pieces and moved each piece on its own. Regardless, in the end, both barns would require a new wall to fill in their open ends.

The maternal branch of the family tree could not have been more different than the paternal side. The McGregors and the Williamsons had immigrated to America in the 1800s from Scotland before moving on again to Canada. As a child, Bessie Pearl McGregor came to Canada with her parents from Dodd City, Arkansas, in the early 1900s. Her father was a carpenter. After her high school education, she met and married Alexander (Alec) Williamson, who had emigrated with his parents from Crested Butte, Colorado. Alec's father was a coal engineer. They settled on a small farm at Lake Thelma southwest of Coronation where, after serving in WWI, Alec earned a living raising and selling draft (work) horses. This was a small profit business back in the '20s, '30s, and '40s, but tractor technology eventually rendered the need for workhorses redundant, turning their farm into a dirt-poor situation.

The Williamson farm remained unchanged for over forty years. There was no electricity, no running water, no sewer or indoor plumbing. The main house consisted of only two rooms, a bedroom and a kitchen/seating area combined, heated by a single wood-burning stove in the main room. Out back stood the outhouse, appropriately named, and a hundred yards away stood the bunkhouse, heated with a single pot-belly woodstove in the middle of one single room.

In an extremely harsh environment, the Williamsons

raised their seven children. Mary, my mother, was the oldest, followed by six boys, who slept in the bunkhouse. In order of age, they were Alex, Ronald, Robert (Mac), David, Cecil, and William (Bill). As a little boy, I would often spend a week or two with my grandparents in the summer. I was the only one of us kids to do so on a regular basis. It was a great holiday. I would ride horses bareback, while holding onto one of my uncles, or explore the little valley of poplar trees. The location they had chosen for the farm was good grassland for raising horses, but the soil was so sandy and arid it was almost not farmable. But, to a little boy, the soil was great for building a small sand house with a little spoon and knife, supposedly put away just for me to use when I was there.

I remember waiting in bed in the morning until the cold linoleum floor heated up enough to walk on with my bare feet. Grandma was always the one who got up first and fired up the woodstove for heat. I remember her freshly baked warm buns, fried chicken, creamy gravy, and fresh new potatoes, peas, and carrots from the garden. The sandy soil may not have been good for grain crops, but it was ideal for growing vegetables.

Grandma never complained about her lot in life, but she must have wondered how she ended up in such a godforsaken place. She had a high school education, a rarity for the time. She gave birth to and reared seven children in the harshest and most minimal of conditions. She never lost her sense of humour, her wise counsel, or her unwavering support of her family, including me.

CHAPTER 3
The Family

The first six years of my life were perfect. Like most children who are blessed to be in a strong family home surrounded by good siblings, my preschool years hold nothing but the best of memories. With the exception of that one incident with Mom and Jean, I do not recall a single time before I was seven that gave me a clue as to what my physical realities really were. Life was truly good.

Time and again, we see evidence of the influence that parents have on their children. Their values and style of communication, discipline, priorities, and work ethics all show up when children become adults. Adults become the product of their childhood environment. I certainly had my share of concern over fairness and some decisions that were taken, or not taken, but they pale in the larger scheme of things. Our parents were excellent role models.

My dad, Alfred Hughes Gillard, which he later changed to Hugh Alfred, was born in Calgary in 1911. He would go on to get his high school education and attend Agriculture College. As a young adult, he experienced the Great Depression before taking over the family farm in the mid '40s. He was a very good-looking man, solidly built, although not overly tall, and always well dressed and proud. He was long on hard work, honesty, and integrity, but short on patience and affection. The latter I believe was due to having lost his siblings, a younger brother and a sister, when he was only a child.

Dad was all business and always paid his share. He would often wait to buy a certain item, but when he did, he bought quality. Our first TV was a Zenith, a very high quality TV at the time, but ironically now long since out of business. Our cars were always Buicks or Oldsmobiles. As for any vices, Dad touched all the bases, but only for short pauses. He would swear a little, have the occasional social drink, and play a little poker, in modest amounts. He had a temper and when his patience ran out, things got corrected, one way or another. I recall at least two instances when his patience ran out with some drunken men.

One time was during the annual Stettler bull sale, where each year we sold five or six of our prized registered Hereford bulls. I was about twelve at the time and we were eating lunch in the arena restaurant when an older man, clearly inebriated, insulted our ranch and bulls. Every patron in the restaurant could hear him and were noticeably embarrassed. Dad quickly became uneasy and then boom! He jumped up, snatched the old man's hat off his head, and slapped him across the face with it, twice. Dad was a proud man who had worked hard to build one of the best Hereford operations in Alberta. I was like the little boy in the movie *Shane*, watching his hero, Alan Ladd, confront the bad guy who had insulted the farmer. Dad was my hero and I was scared and hoping he would win. He did, thankfully. It was over in a second.

The other incident was in the Royal Crown Hotel in our hometown. Jean and I had just seen a movie and were sitting in a cafe booth with Mom, Dad, Grandpa, and Grandma. In the booth behind us sat two guys in their twenties, one of whom was very drunk, or *tight* as it was called back then. He uttered the most profane and vulgar words that would make today's Howard Stern blush—words I had never heard before, for good reason. Everyone was uncomfortable, most of all Dad, who was upset that women and children were hearing such foulness. Dad looked back over his shoulder and gave the guy the "shut up or else" stare. (I later acquired the same style, which friends affectionately termed "The Gill Glare.") It was to no avail; the guy never let up with the profanity. Like the incident at the bull sale, Dad quickly reached his point of no return. He jumped up, walked to the booth, grabbed the guy's nose, twisted it, and said, "Stop that swearing." The guy was so stunned he didn't fight back. The swearing stopped and we all went back to eating our raisin pie *a la mode*, sitting as stunned and quiet as the guy whose nose had just been rearranged without anaesthetic.

Dad was both small a "c" and large "C" conservative. I inherited his "vice in moderation" philosophy of life, his conservatism, his honesty to a fault, high ethics, hardworking standards, and a willingness to contribute to the community. Arguably, I may also have inherited his style of directness and lack of patience. (I'm the guy in the express line counting the items in the person's basket ahead of me.)

I had always looked up to my dad. When I was nine or ten, I recall going out somewhere with him, both of us wearing grey topcoats and tan leather gloves. I felt so proud walking beside him, father and son, identically dressed. I have a hunch that he was proud of me walking beside him, too, but he was never one to show affection. I can't recall our parents being affectionate or saying "I love you." It didn't mean they didn't love us, for they surely did; they were the products of a bygone British era.

My mom, Mary Isabelle (nee Williamson), was from a totally opposite background from Dad. Whereas Dad's parents were English, Mom's were American and Scottish. They lived on a dirt poor farm where hard choices were required when the money wasn't there to fulfill everyone's dreams and aspirations. Mom was able to get her high school education, but unfortunately the same thing was not afforded the boys. They were all bright and ultimately achieved self-made careers in the oil industry despite not having attended university. After graduating from high school, Mom went on to get her teaching degree and taught at least four generations of children. She was the classic old-style teacher—dedicated and committed to the students' learning. Although strict, she earned the respect of her students, so much so that many of her students' classes honoured her when graduating from high school. She taught for fifty years, until she was eighty-five years old. Mom was the approachable one of our parents, the one we went to when we needed money or had a special request to stay at a friend's house. I would always ask Mom first. I preferred to get a "no" from her than Dad and, besides, the odds of success were better.

From Mom I inherited a love of history, politics, an outgoing personality (despite the afflictions), the value of education, and a sense of humour. Some might say that I also got the gift of the gab and a touch of her stubbornness, but that's arguable. This year we celebrate her ninetieth birthday. Like the Energizer Bunny, she is still going strong: volunteering, active in politics, golfing, playing bridge, and enjoying her grandchildren and great-grandchildren.

Geneticists say we get fifty percent of our genes from our father and fifty percent from our mother. Although this may be a proven fact, I'm convinced my dominant genes are on the Williamson side. Cleft features aside, I look and talk like a Williamson. More than anything else though, I have the "Williamson Walk." Check the famous caricature of the Evolution of Man, starting with the ape and progressing up to man, and you'll see me. I'm the second one from the left: bent at the hips, long arms swaying, head reaching my destination well ahead of my body.

My siblings consisted of two older brothers and a younger sister. Irving was eight years older, Stuart was eighteen months older, and Jean, the baby of the family, was one year younger than me.

Irv was the industrious one, a natural at building things and being mechanical. He was good looking, conservative in style, and didn't have a mean bone in his body. He was always tinkering with things and even made us our first lawnmower. He took an old motor from a clothes washer, attached it to a wooden box, and sharpened a piece of metal into a blade. The fact that it had no side protection in case the blade flew off escaped us all. No matter, it was just great to have a power mower. If I were ever stranded on a desert island, I would want Irv there with me.

At only seventeen, Irv joined the Royal Canadian Air Force (RCAF). He eventually married Elaine and enjoyed a successful career, rising to Warrant Officer. He kept the fighter jets, reconnaissance, and search and rescue planes in shape to fly. As kids, we missed Irv a lot when he was gone and always looked forward to him coming home for a visit. I always looked up to Irv and still envy his ability to create things. Irv has always been a solid brother and friend.

Stuart was the child prodigy. He was good looking, bright, funny, athletic, and had tons of personality and confidence. He skipped a grade in school and was definitely "most likely to succeed." He was the president of his high school. He was the first to do "The Twist" at a Coronation high school dance, having seen it the previous week at a dance in Stettler. I remember watching him and feeling immensely proud. "That's *my* brother everyone is watching," I thought. Stuart's natural gift of humour and outgoing personality led him to doing Shelly Berman and Bob Newhart comedy routines on the stage at high school dances. We didn't know it then, but it was a precursor to his career in the entertainment business.

As kids we all had lots of toys, but we always had a funny feeling that Stuart got everything. At age twelve he got a *real* pony. I got a *stick* pony (that's my story and I'm sticking to it). Stuart always had a good sense of humour about the discrepancies, perceived or otherwise. We were reminiscing once about what we played with as kids and I mentioned that I loved pushing this certain toy truck around in the yard. Stuart jokingly replied, "Oh, that's too bad. Mine had a motor." To be fair, Dad all but made him join the 4-H, help break horses, or compete in amateur gymkhana horse races when he would much rather have hung out with his friends and chased girls.

With scholarships in hand, he went to university to become a lawyer, but instead got an Arts degree and pursued acting, writing, and directing. He wrote for Sonny and Cher and the Osmonds before moving on to direct movies for Disney, HBO, and the TV show "Beverly Hills 90210" for many seasons. He is our family's touch of famous. Always supportive and of wise counsel, Stuart did more than anyone to bolster my confidence.

Jean was our bright little star, cute as a button with personality to burn. She was my best buddy growing up. In the summer, we played together endlessly. In the boring winter months, we played Crazy Eights and Go Fish, as well as Sorry or Snakes and Ladders. We learned to jive to 45 rpm records like "Blame it on the Bossa Nova" by Eydie Gorme, "Wake Up Little Susie," by the Everly Brothers, and later to "The Twist" by Chubby Checker.

As a teenager, Jean was incredibly popular—smart, pretty, and nice. In my twenties, I always turned to Jean for advice and support as I entered the dating game, with all the angst, trials, and tribulations of a teenager. Jean helped me pick out my first furniture for my apartment. She was my sister, friend, interior designer, social advisor, and confidante. With her husband, Brian, they built and ran a highly successful electrical business, and if the town ever held a "most popular and respected" contest, Jean would win in a cakewalk. Like our mother and grandmother before her, Jean, being the only daughter, has become the "glue" for all us siblings.

CHAPTER 4
The Old Hometown

Growing up on a ranch didn't mean you didn't have a hometown. Coronation was ours, but the hamlet of Throne was our mailing address. It only had a general store and post office, so it didn't technically qualify as a town. Coronation was where we bought our groceries and farm implements and spent our Saturday nights.

If the written history of our prairies were ever lost, no one would wonder who the primary settlers of the regions were. All the town and village names along the rail line confirm this. It was British through and through. Names were often connected with royalty or the military, like the villages of Fleet, Federal, and Throne; the towns of Coronation, Veteran, Consort, and Loyalist (which stemmed from the coronation year of King George V, in 1911, when the rail line was built east from Stettler).

Coronation was apparently selected by the railway company to be a divisional point and the scene of extensive railway operations, with a route from Chicago to Edmonton. The dirt grades for the north-south intersecting rail lines at Coronation were built, but I'm not sure the rails were ever laid. They certainly weren't there when I grew up.

Economics, I suppose. Another east-west line was built some sixty miles south. It too gave birth to new towns and villages like Hemaruka, so named after the four daughters of the CPR General Manager: Helen, Mary, Ruth, and Kay.

Despite what it looked like on a map, there was actually logic to how much of the prairie was settled. Towns did not simply spring up randomly. There were no natural river crossings or forts that became future town sites. Rather, they arose because of the need for shipping terminals, in the form of grain elevators, beside the rail lines. The collection points that ultimately became towns or hamlets were established about every ten miles, which left a maximum five miles, one way, for a farmer to drive his hitch of horses or oxen to market and return in a day. The farmers were the economic engines that drove the rail company profits. They needed access to supplies and services, thus becoming the lifeline of the small towns. The town, the farmer, and the rail company were all interdependent.

Coronation in the 1950s and '60s was typical of many small towns in western Canada or the US. Its dirt streets, either packed hard by traffic or so muddy people got stuck, could easily have been the movie set for *The Summer of '42*. There was the Chinaman's Cafe, the McFarland Pool Hall, Casey's Barbershop, the Avalon Movie Theatre, the Elks Hall, and the skating and curling rinks. The streets Royal and Windsor were Coronation's equivalent of Broadway and 52nd. On the corner stood the Royal Crown Hotel, three stories high and *the* centre of town, figuratively and literally. To me, it was huge and awe inspiring; nothing rivaled it for height, except for maybe the town water tower. The top two floors held the rooms, including one larger apartment where the owner-manager and his family resided. The main floor consisted of a restaurant, a lobby, and a bar for Men Only. By law, women were not allowed to enter a bar in the 1950s. Banning mixed drinking was a standing principle of the socialist provincial governments that, in reality, were political arms of the conservative right religious population. Later, the laws eased to the point where there was a section for Men Only and a separate section for Ladies and Escorts. Progress was slow on the prairies back then.

Extending out in four different directions from the corner of Royal and Windsor were the hardware store, three grocery stores, one car dealership, a butcher shop (that rented freezer space to families for meat), a newspaper that printed mostly gossip, the creamery, the roundhouse for rail engine repairs, and several grain elevators down by the tracks. The hospital consisted of a two-story wood-framed building, painted white with green trim; the schoolhouse was a two-story red brick building.

One block north of the Royal Crown Hotel, towering two stories high and painted white with black trim, stood The Avalon Theatre. The proprietor, John (Jack) Noonan, also happened to be the town commissioner and a part-time farmer.

He had the highest profile and was *the man about town*. To me, with the exception of my father, they didn't come any more important than Mr. Noonan.

Jack was known for a lot of things, but his most distinguishing feature was his tan felt cowboy hat. Actually, it wasn't the hat so much as how he *wore* the hat—on a sixty-degree angle. Not tilted back like my dad's, but on the corner of his head. He was recognizable from blocks away. It was always a mystery to me how that hat stayed on. I tried duplicating the feat with my own cowboy hat, soon discovering that the only way I could keep it on was to counterbalance the tilt with an equal and opposite tilt of my head. Quite quickly, I put my impressionist career on hold.

As far as us kids knew, the movies at The Avalon were the latest releases. In truth, they were likely well behind the city theatres. No matter. Given the limited options, we always looked forward to the "movie of the week" that ran every Friday, Saturday, and Sunday night, with a Saturday afternoon matinee. High school girls got jobs as ushers—now an extinct species. Jack was the ticket seller—he controlled the big money. Mickey, his son, was the projectionist. Noreen, his daughter, sold the popcorn. Tory, Jack's wife, was a teacher and nowhere to be seen. Movies cost thirty-five cents; popcorn and a small glass bottle of Coke cost ten cents each. There was nothing better than buttered popcorn in a small white bag and a cold Coca-Cola in a glass bottle, right out of the machine. Life was good.

Rarely did a movie play that at least one empty Coke bottle wasn't tipped over, supposedly accidentally. It would roll down the floor under rows and rows of seats, clanging off the metal seat stands as it made its way to the front, like a pinball machine. Mercifully, someone would figure out that the bottle was coming from behind and reach down and grab it as it passed underneath. If the bottle made it to the front, someone made a silent motion of victory. For movies that dragged, *this* was the highlight.

By any measure, The Avalon was a big theatre, seating about 200 patrons on a gentle slope from back to front. One year, Jack installed all new seats of the newest and latest design available, but with one unique feature. On the end of every third row was a "loveseat," a wider single seat designed for two. This revolutionary design, conceived in a moment of romantic brilliance by some furniture designer, quickly became a complete failure. The novelty wore off and the impracticalities of the concept became evident. Other than the true lovers who were willing to be publicly tagged as such, who would sit in the seats? Inevitably the fat lady, the old maid, the unkempt man, or the kid with the cough parked themselves in the seat first. But this was a good thing—unless the movie sold out. Then a real-life game of musical chairs ensued as everyone tried to avoid getting the unoccupied half of the loveseat. People would race up and down aisles looking for anything *but that* seat. Even the hated middle seats became sought after. Like a miracle at an evangelical meeting, those with canes were all of a sudden able to run and near-sighted people were suddenly happy sitting in the back row. Oral Roberts would have been proud.

Going to the movies was something we always looked forward to. They were our link to the outside world and dreams. If the weather was good, we'd head in Friday or Saturday evening after the chores were done. Bad weather usually meant seeing a matinee. As much as we looked forward to going to the movies, we dreaded asking for money to pay for it. If we were lucky, Mom had enough cash for all of us, for she had a soft spot and a healthy touch of generosity when it came to doling out money. Her movie money came without the interrogation. No questions asked. But, God forbid, if she happened to not have the cash, then the most painful of all money transactions would take place.

"You'll have to go ask your dad," she would say.

There was *never* a good time to ask Dad for money and we would stall as long as we could. But time was our enemy. We had to ask before getting into the car. Dressed up and sitting in the kitchen, looking like three little waifs, we would wait for Dad to finish getting ready. The kitchen was the self-chosen altar of sacrifice. He had to go through the kitchen to get from the bedroom to the front door. In my mind, it was as good a place as any to die. We took turns asking, but for some reason I seemed to always draw the short straw.

"Dad," I'd squeak as he strutted through. "Could we have some money for the movie?"

He would abruptly stop, a grimace on his face, obviously disappointed that he hadn't made it past us. "Well, how much do you need?"

He'd start pulling his black folded leather wallet out of his back pocket, the kind complete with a built-in coin pocket and snap. Standing over the grey chrome kitchen table, he would start the process. He would first take out a quarter, followed by two dimes, and drop each on the table before sliding them over, one at a time, in slow motion.

"Is that enough?" he'd ask.

"No," I'd whisper, thinking if I talked softly he would respond softly.

"Why?"

"I'd like to buy a pop and popcorn."

"How much more?"

"Ten cents." It felt like I was asking for the entire proceeds of his prize bull.

Out would come two more nickels that I quickly slid across the table towards me and into my other hand. "Thanks."

Then it was Jean or Stuart's turn at getting money out of the wallet made of stone. But they had it easy. By then, Dad knew how much each kid needed. They got to skip over the begging part. Call it paranoia, but I'm convinced they often got a whole dollar bill because I had taken all his exact change for the first fifty-five cents.

The fact that evening movies usually started at seven and nine o'clock was irrelevant. Mom and Dad were oblivious to movie start times. To them, movies would simply have to wait until the chores were done, including milking the cows. Often, we would get dropped off at The Avalon around eight o'clock, which meant that we would walk into the theatre halfway through the first movie that had started an hour earlier. In total darkness, we'd split up, each of us trying to find our friends, disrupting the patrons as we worked our way down the middle of the rows to an empty seat.

At the end of the first movie, the lights would come on and everyone would get up and leave, except the Gillard kids. We'd change seats to sit beside those friends who came to the second movie, watch the news and cartoons, and then watch the first half of the same movie. Halfway through, the Gillard kids would stand up from different parts of the theatre and work their way out and to the back. Not surprisingly, the first half of the movie often didn't excite us that much when we had already seen the ending. Knowing that Janet Leigh died in the shower sort of took the excitement out of the beginning of *Psycho*.

The post-movie routine was always the same. We would meet in the lobby and trek down to the Royal Crown Hotel, where Mom and Dad, and usually Grandma and Grandpa, would be drinking coffee and waiting for all of us to arrive. There was one occasion when this routine was broken, when I was about seven or eight. Jean, Stuart, and Irv met up with

Mom and Dad at the hotel. Sometime later, someone asked, "Where's Dougie?" Suddenly, it dawned on everyone that I was missing. Today you'd call the police, put out an Amber Alert, and form a volunteer search party, all hoping for the best but expecting the worst.

The kid must be somewhere nearby, they thought. How long they looked for me, I don't know, but after scouring the entire hotel and the streets nearby, someone threw out the idea that just maybe I was still in the theatre. The Avalon was completely dark and locked up, so they drove to Jack Noonan's home to see if he would come down and unlock the theatre to check for a missing child.

I recall the moment I woke up in the middle seat near the front and saw Mr. Noonan standing in the aisle, looking down the row of seats at me. "Yup, he's here," he said. I had fallen asleep during the movie. No one had bothered to wake me or check to see if there was someone still in the theatre when it came time to shut out the lights and lock up for the night. I can only imagine how I would have panicked if I had awoken in total darkness and been unable to find my way out. So much for sibling stick-togetherness.

CHAPTER 5

School Days

Throne had a population less than ten, situated about ten miles east of Coronation. It consisted of two grain elevators, a general store with gas pumps, a one-room school, and four houses, all within yards of the rail line. Our ranch was located about two miles to the southeast. At Throne, we got our mail, bought small groceries and supplies, delivered our grain to market, and got part of our education.

The Throne school was a small white building with green trim and it was the centre of my universe. A shed stood outside where students tied their horses. Inside, it held twenty tiny desks, row on row, with inkwells and wooden tops that could be lifted to store books inside. Heated only by a wood stove, it hosted the box socials, the rural dances, the children's Christmas parties, election voting booths, and whatever else was needed. It was the social centre for the rural farms and families and the half dozen or so Throne residents.

Stuart and Irv were already attending the school when it came my turn to take the first step to years of educational enlightenment. In the fall and spring, they rode two miles of gravel road to and from school on bikes, the old fashioned kind with no gears or brakes, and then back again. I didn't have a bike of my own, which sometimes was a blessing, and sometimes not. If I could get a ride to school, that was fine with me.

In his infinite wisdom, Dad had decided that Irv, then only fourteen, would take me to school on the back of his bike. This decision was one of many that, in my mind, was harsh and unfair to Irv. Irv constructed a metal seat behind his for me to sit on for the four mile roundtrip. Once the flat piece of six-inch wide metal was hammered, bent, and twisted into shape, it was braced horizontally above the rear wheel and ready for test trials. Years later, Irv would question how little effort it would have taken, had anyone thought it through, to build me little footrests so I didn't have to ride with both legs sticking straight out sideways for two miles. Certainly, Irv could not be blamed; to have even built the seat at his age was incredible. Even today, I couldn't have done better than he did.

Notwithstanding that the trek to school took half an hour, somebody had the brilliant idea that I should learn to jump onto the seat while the bike was moving, all in the interest of shaving three seconds off the thirty minute trip, I suppose. If the objective wasn't to save time, it surely must have been to make it easier for Irv to carry me than starting from a dead stop with added weight on the bike.

So, on a hot 1954 August prairie night, in the middle of the hard-packed dirt yard, the next great transportation test trial occurred. Like a Roman gladiator in the middle of the Coliseum, facing certain death from the circling chariot, I stood at the ready—four feet high and fifty pounds—as Irv circled on his bike. With the siblings cheering and no doubt hoping for a wreck, I ran as fast as I could in a tight circle, parallel to the moving bike, holding on to the "built-for-me" seat, and then taking the great leap of faith. The first effort was too low and I fell, bouncing, scraping, and flipping to the ground. The second attempt was too high and I fell to the other side with the same result. The third attempt was a perfect landing. One small step for man, but one giant leap for me! I had just passed my first lesson in perseverance.

Mrs. Brightland was my Grade One teacher. She was also Stuart's, Irv's, and everyone else's teacher! The entire first grade sat in row one, seat one—me. She didn't ask my name, as she and everyone else within a five-mile radius already knew of little Dougie Gillard. I was famous!

I was the Grade One class. Little Shirley was the Grade Two class, situated immediately behind me. To my real comfort, Stuart sat behind her, already in Grade Four after skipping Grade Three. Stuart made it really handy for me to get up and wander back, at will, to get help. He was only eight years old, but to me he was an adult and always had the answers to my most challenging questions. He was so smart, he knew the answer to, "What comes after C?" Even at such a young age, Stuart would always stop what he was doing to help me.

Irv was at least four rows over and five desks back. If I stood up and tilted my head just the right way, I could see him.

It was too risky to walk the maze and try to get to him. This was a good thing, as no doubt he was still recovering from the gruelling bike ride with my fifty pounds of unbalanced weight behind, holding on to him and complaining all the way.

Being the only student in Grade One had its advantages. I graduated at the top of my class. I was a confident seven-year-old ready to move up to the next grade. Oh, happy days!

Bob Dylan's 1960s song containing the words "The times they are a-changin'," comes to mind when I think of how the rural areas of the country changed back in the early 1950s. As it turned out, my year in Grade One was the final year for our little country school. In the name of efficiency, the school division determined that all small country schools were to be permanently closed and all students were to be bussed to bigger town schools; in our case, Coronation.

As a seven-year-old, I knew *change* meant something different, but like all young children, what change really entailed never concerned me. In fact, I don't recall any conversation beforehand about changing schools. The whole thing was news to me.

So, on the first September school day of 1955, Irv, Stuart, Jean, and I walked up our red shale lane to the main gravel road. With my Roy Rogers lunchbox in hand (a homegrown tomato and lettuce sandwich inside, with wax paper between the bread and tomato slices to keep the bread from becoming soggy), we waited for our first-ever school bus ride. We were nervous farm kids heading to the great unknown.

In the distance, we could see a small yellow speck moving along the gravel road toward us, dust kicking up from behind like the spray of a speedboat. What looked like a yellow police paddy wagon stopped at our lane. The door opened and the driver said, "Good morning." It was Vern Bishell, the proprietor of the Throne General Store and Gas Station. He had obviously jumped at the chance to supplement his income by driving the school bus. Mr. Bishell was a familiar sight on a scary day.

Our personal paddy wagon held about a dozen of our former schoolmates from the one-room schoolhouse. Everyone sat in bench-style seats that ran down the sides and across the end in a U-shape. It was first-come, first-served, so the end seats facing forward were always taken by the time we got on.

To me, everything was overwhelming: new school, new class, new teacher, new fellow pupils. I was scared and nervous, as all kids from the Throne school were, as I got off the school bus and didn't know where to go. Nowadays, doting parents take their kids to the first year of junior high, senior high, and even university to "be there for them" on their first day. I was seven with very distinctive features, attending a strange school, and had no one with me. Many years later, I asked Mom why she didn't come with me, or any of us, for that matter. She answered, "I suggested to Dad that I take you, but he said there was no need." Being raised and treated like any other kid, without favouritism, was probably one of the keys to making it on my own and eventually having a successful career. But, in this case, Dad took normalcy too far. I could have used some help.

I didn't know where to go, but I remember showing a piece of paper to a much older and taller girl, who looked down at me and said, "Oh, Grade Two. Go in through that door over there." Somehow, like the others, I managed to find the right classroom and pick out a desk in row three and four seats back.

Mrs. Beatty was my teacher. Her previous vocation must have been Nazi prison camp guard. She had jet-black hair, black glaring eyes, and a goose step to go along with it. When she entered the room, everyone became dead silent.

With a loud clap of her hands, she barked, "Okay, everyone, time for roll call. State your name, starting with you over there," and she pointed to the little girl in the first seat in the first row.

State my name? This was new to me. No one had told me about this. There was no roll call in Throne. Even though I had never spoken my name to strangers and didn't have a clue how I spoke, I was very nervous. It's amazing how small children have intuitive skills about certain things.

The little girl in seat one, row one, stood up, said her name, and then sat down. The roll call had commenced. Each kid stood up and stated his or her name, sat down, and the next one behind immediately stood up. They had done this before!

A single wave of real-life Dominoes took off, going up the first row, jumping across to the back of the second row, down to the front, and then over to the third, and on it went. My heart raced as the wave neared, for in an instant it would be my turn. For the first time I had to say my name in public. For some unexplainable reason, I seemed to know that this couldn't be good.

"Nudnass Niller," I said shyly, with no distinctive emphasis on any letter or syllable.

"What did you say? I can't hear you!" She tapped the ruler on the inside of her open palm, prepared for further action if necessary.

"Nudnass Niller," I repeated loudly.

"I can't understand you. Say it again!" She was now marching towards me.

Again I tried, louder and with tears welling up in my eyes. "Nudnass Niller." Standing there with all the others watching, I felt so alone. It was excruciatingly painful.

"Just my luck. I get a kid who can't even say his own name," she mumbled before pointing to the next kid to restart the process. (I am convinced that she also said "so stupid," but I'll give her the benefit of the doubt.)

Scared, hurt, and embarrassed, I sat down, laid my head on my crossed arms, and cried. I had gone from being happy and confident to sad and insecure in an instant. There was no compassion there. There was no Mrs. Brightland who knew me and no brother Stuart two desks back. I was on my own. At that moment, all my confidence was zapped. Not just for a few days, but for many years. That teacher's single act of non-compassion triggered years of self-doubt. Fortunately, my confidence returned, although progress was measured one grade at a time. With only one exception, my grades improved every year through elementary, junior, and senior high and university, culminating in my highest marks the year I graduated with an undergraduate degree.

For years, I resented how she treated me that first day of Grade Two, but the passage of time softens one's views, I suppose. She wouldn't have had any exposure to someone like me and no experience handling "challenged" children. Still, where was the common sense? Even a little sympathy would have made a huge difference.

The other thing I discovered in Grade Two was that I didn't have a right side of the brain, figuratively speaking. I was all left side. I could add two plus two and get four, *and* a gold star, but when it came to being creative, I had nothing. Once, the class art project was to transform red tissue paper into a carnation by folding, pressing, and twisting it onto a wire. Mine resembled a dried up red onion, which generated muffled laughs and whispers.

When I look at my Grade Two school picture I see a small, unhappy boy. Upon closer observation, however, I notice my homemade haircut (I must have been Mom's first test run), so, on further thought, maybe that was the *real* problem. My cleft lip and crooked teeth paled in comparison to my haircut.

Meeting people is all visual at first. Life is such a visual thing. Personality comes second. People who have facial disfigurements, like burn or accident victims, know this all too well. Clefted people, children and adults, are no different. The temptation to take the easy route and become withdrawn is very high. Family support is critical, but ultimately it is one's inner self that makes the difference between going forward or backwards. To go forward requires confidence and a willingness to ignore the bad and move on as if all was normal.

It is a fact of life that kids tease each other. They may not mean any harm, but what they say is often cruel and has long-lasting results. No exceptions were made for me. I was often asked, "What happened to your face?" or "Why do you talk so funny?" Being mean is not exclusive to children. Adults can be just as mean, if not more, and they know better. One time, a mother was walking with her child and pulled the child over by the arm and asked me, "Hey kid, what happened to you? Were you hit by a hockey puck?" "No," I replied, "I had an operation." At just eight years old, I had somehow developed a non-emotional response. However, I remember sticking up for myself once, when a young kid kept staring at me from a booth in a restaurant, with the silent approval of his mother. "If you stare long enough, you'll go blind," I told him. He blinked and looked away, as did his mother, unapologetically. The stares diminished somewhat over time as I became "known in town," but they never really ended until my mid-twenties.

I must have twins all over the country. To this day, a complete stranger will approach me and say, "I know you. Where did we meet before?"

I'll reply, "I'm sorry, but I don't think we've ever met."

"No, I'm sure I've met you. You grew up in Fort St. John, didn't you?"

"I've never lived in Fort St. John or even been there. I think you're confusing me with someone else."

"Well, you must have a twin brother. You look exactly like someone I know."

This incident has repeated itself many times in my life. Now, I know this happens to thousands of people all the time, but what is it about some people who think cleft-lipped people are all identical twins? I would guess that people with Down Syndrome experience similar recognition confusion. Heaven forbid if a cleft-lipped man commits a violent crime. I'll be hauled off to a police lineup, where the victim will surely point to me and say, "That's him! That's the guy who mugged me!" I hope I have an alibi.

Bullying today is a serious social issue. There were bullies back in our day as well, they just weren't identified as such. Then, it was more a fact of life and largely ignored. Not surprisingly, I was bullied, but not as often as I could have been; a fact I attribute to the rural and small town values where I grew up.

One of the worst incidents I witnessed did not involve me, but rather my uncle. Mom's youngest sibling was much younger than her and not that much older than us kids. Uncle Bill was a good teenage kid, straight off the farm, shy, and easily intimidated. One day while heading to my bus after school, I saw Bill and could tell something was wrong. A bunch of boys were blocking the door of Bill's bus and one was taunting him. "Why don't you wear your glasses?" Bill wore glasses, but must have felt uncomfortable about how they looked so he often kept them off. The bully was verbally and physically intimidating him into putting his glasses on. Bill was surrounded and clearly embarrassed and scared, but he wasn't backing down.

Time was on Bill's side. Eventually, everyone broke away to catch his or her own bus, so no fight actually ensued. It was a classic case of bullying. Stuart witnessed it all, too, and many years later he and I would speak of the incident and how awful we felt about it. Stuart regrets to this day not stepping in and saying something to the bully, who was a classmate of his.

Some people surprise, like a boy named Frankie. He and his brother were the *real* town bullies and surely at the top of the town's Most Wanted list. Everyone was scared silly of them, with their leather jackets, ducktail combs, and wallets with chains. They walked the talk. My near-death encounter with them occurred when I was only seven years old. I was peeing into the urinal in the boys' washroom, a long metal trough that sloped gently down from the right to left, where it drained out. Frankie came up and stood beside me to do his thing. I was so nervous. I kept my eyes down and tried to pee faster. Before I could walk away, he was done and caught up to me. This had all the makings of an easy hit.

He looked at me and said, "Hey! You talk funny. You have that scar on your lip because you had an operation, didn't you?" I nodded. "Okay," he said and walked away. This conversation would have meant nothing to most people, but to me it meant a lot. He had uncharacteristically asked me, maybe even with a hint of compassion, if I had what he thought I had. Better yet, I was off his hit list of kids to beat up. My non-emotional response had sufficed. Coming from such an unlikely source, the conversation showed me that sometimes the most likely don't always do the likeliest things. (Stuart was always convinced Frankie and his friends had stolen the hubcaps off his car, so maybe our amateur criminal profiling was correct.)

When I was in my late teens, a six-foot-four farm kid named Terry often embarrassed me at the local town hall dances. It was common for all the guys to stand as a group in the back of the hall. I was still very short and skinny for my age, so it was easy for Terry to sneak up behind me, squeeze his hands around my neck, and lift me straight up, feet dangling a foot above the floor. He'd hold me there for a few seconds.

Other than the missing rope, this was capital punishment by hanging. To him, it was a joke, but to me it was painful and humiliating. I regret not turning around just once and kicking him in the most vulnerable spot. It would have been only once, as I'm sure I would have needed facial reconstruction again.

My scholastic collapse from the Grade One high to the Grade Two low was monumental. I didn't really pass Grade Two; I was *moved on*. I should have failed, but Mrs. Beatty wanted to move the problem on to Mrs. Sims, the Grade Three teacher. My Grade Two report card has gone missing, but I don't recall getting anything above a D or C. I'm pretty sure there had to be some Fs on it somewhere.

A funny thing happened on the first day of school in Grade Three. There was the same roll call, the same domino process, but this time when I said, "Nudlas Niller," the girl in front of me said, "His name is Douglas Gillard." Like the friends of Spartacus, from all over the room, others spontaneously chimed in, "Douglas Gillard." They had been ready for just this moment. No one told them to do it; they just did it. They had not only gotten to know me in Grade Two, but also began to see me for who I really was, just a young boy yearning to be like them. So, instead of insecurity and tears, my face lit up with a smile. For the first time, I discovered that I had real friends. The little boy with crooked teeth, a droopy lip, and a bad scar actually had friends! They liked me for who I was! For several years thereafter, whenever we had a new teacher who had never met me, the same supportive ritual would occur. My dreaded fears on the first day of school were over.

The remaining years of elementary school were as close to normal as I could expect. I was growing more confident and at ease with each passing year, despite not improving my speech one iota. With no speech therapy, I struggled with communication. As time passed, everyone got used to how I talked and seemed to instantly translate the words I had trouble with.

If there was a bright side, it was that there was no discrimination, at least not then. I was not excluded from anything for "talking funny." When the Grade Five class stood on the school gym stage for the Christmas concert, I was there, although Mr. Wager struggled with where to position me in the choir. Should I be in the soprano or bass section? There was no *nasal* section. By a process of elimination, he eventually found the right place for me. I stood proudly in the girls' section, belting out "Silen Nide" and "Har, the Haro Angels Sig." I was one of them and proud of it. Thankfully, he didn't choose "The Twelve Days of Christmas," for I hate to think how "Six geese a-laying" would have come out of my mouth.

When it came to public speaking, I too had to participate. I hated the idea initially, but it actually bolstered my confidence and confirmed to me that I was just a normal kid, at least on the inside. Not being creative or a natural orator conveniently led me to be better at researching and writing. My chosen topics were as simple as they were diverse, ranging from the duckbilled platypus to Abraham Lincoln. Mr. Wager must have graded me on content and style and not on enunciation, because I passed. I still have my report card that shows me getting a B+ on Oral Reading and an A+ on Silent Reading. How does one assess Silent Reading? Reading without following the words with one's fingers?

The important "take-away" for me singing in the Christmas choir and speaking in public was that I was treated as *normal*. No favours asked or given and, more importantly, no bypassing because of speech. This contributed greatly to my modus operandi of living and acting as if I was no different than anyone else. Discrimination would show its ugly side in the early part of my career, but the inclusiveness of my teachers, with the one notable exception of Mrs. Beatty, gave me much confidence as to how I should conduct myself in the world, regardless of what others think. It was a small but invaluable show of support.

Public speaking would later become sort of a roadmap of life as I aged. In my late twenties, as the head of a service club, I started speaking at various functions and later had the honour of being master of ceremonies for two friends and a nephew at their weddings. Later yet, I gave speeches at large conferences in the oil industry. Now, sadly, as a true sign of aging, I'm giving tributes and eulogies.

CHAPTER 6
Reality Check

My maternal grandmother was always trying to instill confidence in me. She had raised seven children in a two-room house and bunkhouse, with no electricity, no running water, and an outhouse. The children all went different ways as adults and had varying degrees of success, but she always treated them the same and held each one in equal esteem.

My special bond with her had really started when I was about eight or nine. One evening in Coronation, Mom, Grandma, and I were in the car. I sat in the backseat and overheard Mom say, "I wonder if he will ever marry?" Without hesitation, Grandma said, "Well, absolutely, Mary. He'll get married someday." Neither knew that I could hear them, but what I heard became forever locked into my memory. I would often reflect on their short but telling conversation. The question didn't hurt my feelings. I didn't really grasp the magnitude of Mom's concern and I recall thinking, "Why wouldn't I get married?"

Veteran was the nearest village to the east of our ranch and, during the winter, Stuart, Jean, and I would sit and watch

Mom and Dad curl in the Veteran curling rink. The kitchen was upstairs and built like a diner, with small tables and maybe six stools at the counter. Curling volunteers would cook hamburgers, fries, pies, sandwiches, and soup for those watching the curling and for the curlers themselves when they were finished their game. All proceeds went to the Curling Club.

As I sat down at the counter to order, I looked up and there she was. Behind the counter, wearing an apron and ready to take my order, was a lady with a scar and a nasal voice just like mine. I had trouble understanding her. It was true role reversal. I now knew what I looked like to others. I had discovered that I was not alone, but to see someone with the same thing shocked me.

"Is that what I sound like? Is that what I look like?" I thought. For the first time, I saw and heard what others saw and heard with me. And the weirdest feeling of all was that I looked at her as "different," as if I was the normal one. Because we lived in a small rural community, she no doubt already knew of me, but I knew nothing of her. She was nice and *married* with two children.

CHAPTER 7
Life on the Ranch

Upon retirement in the late 1940s to the coast of British Columbia, Tom and Ethel Gillard handed the farm down to our father, their only surviving son of three children. If you hated cattle, it was a farm. If you loved cattle, it was a ranch. In reality, ours was a hybrid with both cattle and grain, but in our hearts it was a ranch.

Mom and Dad named it "By The Way Ranch," leaving no doubt which way they leaned. Grain farming was necessary to not only feed the cattle, but also to provide a diversified income. Over the years, through buying and leasing, they acquired over 3,000 acres of land and became quite successful.

Our ranch was a true working ranch, not some small acreage within a big city limit with one lonely horse in a steel corral. Mom and Dad had a true passion for raising registered purebred Polled and Horned Hereford cattle and owning Quarter horses. When they retired in 1964 and had a dispersal sale, over 150 head of cows, bulls, and steers were sold. By today's standards, with the massive consolidation of farms, this would not be that large, but back in the '50s and '60s on the prairie where we lived, the By The Way was considered one of the largest and finest ranches.

There's nothing like springtime on the prairies. Snow melting, water running, crocuses blooming, gophers coming out of their winter sleep, and, best of all, new baby calves. It was a wondrous time for me. The new calves, with their clean white faces, would sometimes play by running in one direction with their tails straight up in the air. Then, as if by some magic signal, they would all stop simultaneously, stand still for a couple of seconds, and then change direction and run again before each heading back to their mothers.

As a little boy, branding the calves each late summer was one of my favourite times. Dad always made sure Stuart and I had jobs to do. Long gone were the days of roping the calf in the field and dragging it over to the fire to be branded, vaccinated, and other things. After herding the cows and calves a few miles back to the ranch, we would lock them in the corral overnight. The next day, the calves would be separated out and put in a special pen with a "squeeze" chute at the end. The hired man would chase one calf at a time into the chute and my job was to "pull the rope" on the squeeze as soon as his head poked through. In my young mind, I had *the* most important job!

When he wasn't helping chase the calves into the chute, Stuart helped Mom keep the branding irons hot on the propane fire, handing them to Dad as needed. Our brand was a backward "G" followed by a "T" with a quarter circle arc just above. The "G" and the "T" were Tom Gillard's initials, spelled backwards. When the three hot irons were pressed onto the calf's hide, he would let out a bellow of pain. It was a necessary evil of ranching, but I always felt sorry for the calf. Once it was branded and vaccinated, Dad would nod his head and that was my signal to release the squeeze, open the door, and let the calf run out. Given the hell they had just been through, it was little wonder that not a single calf balked at leaving the chute. If the calf was a heifer or good-looking bull calf, then its ordeal was over. However, if the calf was an unlucky bull calf of less than top quality, his ordeal was by no means over. With a rope around his neck, he would exit the chute until he reached the end of the rope. He would be taken down to the ground and stretched out on his side for one more piece of necessary business—making him into a steer! The calf must have thought, "Which is the worst of two evils? The pain of the hot irons or the knife slicing my prairie oysters?" This was his day from hell, for sure.

The next day, we would herd the cows and their calves back to their grazing pasture until fall. In the fall, we would reverse the trail process, but this time to wean the calves from their mothers. I recall laying awake all night listening to the calves and their mothers bawling for each other. The calves would be separated into three corrals, one for heifers (females), one for steers (the unlucky), and one for the bull calves. The mothers would be returned to another pasture for the winter and then calve again in the spring. And the whole process would be repeated.

Of course, a ranch is not a real ranch unless there's breaking of horses involved. Dad had broken horses for years, but once Stuart was in his late teens, he was deemed man enough to get on the horse. Dad's method was straight out of the Old West, long before the "Horse Whisperer's" gentle, take your time and build trust approach. Years ago, before there were chutes at rodeos to hold the horses for the rider to mount, the broncs were snubbed up to another rider and horse in the middle of the arena. As soon as the contestant climbed into the saddle his horse would be released and the bronc ride would start. Dad was from the old school. He would tightly wrap the bronc's halter rope on his saddle horn and then instruct Stuart, "Okay, get on him now." The look of sheer terror on Stuart's face said it all. He would rather have had a lobotomy than get on that horse. Once he was in the saddle and had grabbed the reins, the By The Way amateur rodeo began! Stuart's horse would buck and pull away, while Dad's horse would recall old memories of when he was young and try bucking, too. I was scared just watching while sitting on the corral fence. Amazingly, no one was killed in all the chaos. Little wonder though that Stuart chose to leave the ranch when he got older. It was that or risk dying young.

Lucky for me, I was too young to die on a bronc back then. Later, after we moved to Okotoks, I had to take my turn at "being a man." My bronc-riding career lasted less than eight seconds. One ride and nobody had to tell me twice what I wasn't good at it.

When I think back to the old home place, now completely gone, we kids didn't appreciate the commitment our parents made to keep the ranch spiffy compared to others around us. They took great pride in the ranch. The house was white with red trim, the two barns were red with green roofs, and the picket fences were white. There were solid wooden corrals, a driveway of red shale, lots of trees on the north side for wind protection, and the sign. *The sign* was four feet by six and made of wood. It stood at the front entrance of the lane into the farm and read "BY THE WAY RANCH" painted in the shape of an arch at the top, with Hugh Gillard neatly printed on the bottom left hand corner. A painting of a Hereford bull's face stared out from the middle, reflecting the same pride we all felt.

Neighbours communicated either by driving or telephone. The telephone was encased in a wooden box screwed to the wall. It had a handheld receiver, a separate microphone to speak into, and a handle on the side for ringing up the neighbour. There were no telephone lines or even telephone companies back then. Barbed wire fence connected the telephones. Our telephone was wired out of the house and onto the barbed wire fence in the back. All the neighbours were connected this way, sort of like a mini AT&T co-op. If anyone left the wrong gate open on their fence, the whole system was in jeopardy. Everyone's phone would ring at the same time when someone dialed a neighbour, but each had their own distinctive Morse code-type ring. A *short* ring was only four or five bell tolls, lasting about one or two seconds, and a *long* ring would last maybe three or four seconds. One farmer's "number" would be two longs, another long and a short, and yet another two shorts and a long. When the phone rang, everyone knew by the code who it was for. Our phone number was three shorts. There was an honour system in place, given that the entire system was a party line, so of course no one listened in on others' conversations. Right? Mom always suspected one old lady listened in every time because she could hear her breathing.

Although I never knew it at the time—no one ever does, growing up in the 1950s on the prairies—I witnessed a tremendous transition from the romantic to the mechanized way of doing things. The old ways were rapidly disappearing and I consider myself lucky to have seen the "way it used to be." Our four black Percheron horses—Dolly, Chub, May, and Darky—did the heavy pulling of plows, reaper binders, wagons, hay racks, and whatever else needed pulling. Soon, they were gone, replaced by John Deere and Ford tractors. I remember the oat bundles that the "bundler" had cut and tied. Dad and our hired hand then used a pitchfork to stack them into neat stooks of six or more sheaves each. This kept the grain heads off the ground to stay dry.

I remember what must have been our last, or close to last, use of a threshing machine. As a little boy, I thought there was something majestic and awe inspiring about this huge grey machine that ate the oat bundles and then spit out grain and leftover straw. The threshing machine was a technological marvel that gave way to an even greater marvel: the combine. It circled the field, pulled or driven, cutting and separating the grain and spitting the straw out the rear end. Gone were the high straw stacks from the threshing machines that stood as sentinels watching over the field during winter. Horses and cows fed on the straw stacks at their pleasure, chewing their way in from the bottom and creating one giant mushroom-like structure. At some point, gravity took over when the stem got so thin that the top would collapse on itself. I always wondered if it would kill the cow or horse feeding under it. I guess not, for to the best of my knowledge no cow ever died eating a straw pile.

When it came to changing technology, the handling of hay was not exempt from progress. The loose hay piled in huge stacks gave way to mechanized balers that scooped up the rows of loose cut grass and magically churned out rectangular bale after rectangular bale, each tightly tied by two strings of tough baler twine. Dad had one of the first balers in the country, a red New Holland. I used to stand on a sled pulled behind the New Holland, stacking the massive bales as they came spitting out. The bale could be adjusted for ease of handling, but Dad always set the dial at the max. Maybe he was bent on saving twine, but I swear the bales came out four feet long and weighing a ton each.

I hated grain farming. It was boring, dirty, and void of all fun. Each year, the same ritual ensued: plant the crops of wheat, oat, and barley, and start praying. Pray for rain. Pray for the grasshoppers to stay away. Pray for a nice fall to harvest the crop. Pray for good grain prices. There was enough praying material to hold our own two-day tent revival meeting. "We ain't askin' much, Lord, but we'd be mighty grateful if you could deliver on these four simple requests." More often than not, the Lord didn't seem to hear too well. Usually, it was the rain that never came or, if it did, it came too little and too late. Dad managed risk by spreading the crops around the country, thus reducing the likelihood of getting totally wiped out by hail at any one time. By The Way Ranch managed risk before hedge funds.

When I was young, Dad took me with him to the blacksmith shop to heat and bend a piece of steel bar into its former shape. I held one end up while the blacksmith heated the other end. Out of nowhere he asked me, in a purposeful and non-complimentary way, "You must be one of those Olmulski kids. You look like an Olmulski." The Olmulskis were a large family of twelve children, poor and not well educated, who lived three miles from our farm. They were good and hardworking people, but not exactly *Farm and Ranch Journal* cover material. I knew what he meant and why he said it: to get in a jab at Dad. Dad glared at him. With his quick temper and fatherly instincts, he wanted to slug the guy but held back, presumably until at least the pipe was fixed. When the job was all but done, my end of the pipe fell out of my hands. The other end, much heavier and hotter, immediately dropped onto the blacksmith's foot. The man screamed. "Sorry," I said.

Dad paid the bill and we drove back to the farm. I knew the blacksmith's hurtful utterance burned inside him. We drove along in silence, both of us looking straight ahead, afraid to look at each other.

After a couple of miles of silence, I said, "I dropped the pipe on purpose."

Calmly and softly, still looking straight ahead, he said, "You did?"

I nodded.

He said nothing else, but I could see him grinning. He was a proud man and I knew he was pleased. Dad and I bonded a bit that day.

When you grow up on a farm, you don't get to choose your chores. People in authority allocate the workload. The boys got the outside jobs and Jean helped with the cooking. I dreaded the fall season because it was grain harvesting time. With apologies to Dickens, "It was the best of times, it was the worst of times" for kids on a farm. Filling the granaries with wheat, barley, or oats was bad enough, but the worst was storing the "chop" for later use as livestock feed. The first part of the chop process was simple and non-threatening. The oat bundles were fed into a chopper, power driven by conveyor belts on a flywheel of a running tractor. The second part was a little more dangerous. The chopper's whirling blades would instantly convert the sheaves into a fine oat material—the "chop"—which would then shoot up a chimney-type pipe at rocket speed to the top of the granary, and then drop down in the hole.

Granaries resembled a small house of about ten feet long, six feet wide, and ten feet high, with a peaked roof. Constructed of solid wood, granaries only had two portals: one on the side, to take the product out as needed; and one at the very top, cut into the peaked roof for pouring the grain into but capped the rest of the time. Granaries were one hundred percent about practicality and zero percent about safety. The chop followed the simple laws of physics. Fed in from the top, the chop dropped to the floor, piled up in a cone, and spread out to the sides. As the pile grew higher, it eventually reached the sides and then filled up vertically. Eventually, the volcano of chop reached the top, but since the granary was still only half full, a solution was needed. To ensure there was not a single square inch of room not filled with chop, someone had to go in and spread the stuff around to the sides with a shovel, while it continued to pour in. This was where the little people came in and I was one of the little people. When Britain passed the child labour laws for coal mines in the 19th century, they should have included the "chop houses" in the colonies as well.

I hated going into the granary to shovel chop. If I could have run away as soon as I saw the cone of chop coming out the top, I would have. Where was the Underground Railroad when I needed it? Dad wasn't mean, at least not intentionally. This is why farm kids were put on the earth.

Once the chop started falling through the top, continuous and non-stop, a real sense of anxiety set in. The total darkness, the noise of the auger, and the dust all worked to convince me I was going to die, smothered to death, and not found until they took the feed out during the next winter. Chop had to be the inspiration for Agent Orange, just a different colour. Our chop might not have been dropped from a plane, but in all other aspects it was identical. One had two choices: shovel or die. I learned quickly how to make a decision—shovel!

There are shovels and then there are shovels. By the 1960s, lightweight aluminum shovels had arrived on the market to make it easier to do just this kind of work. Dad would have none of it. Quality to him meant buying things that would last and shovels were no different. It would be heavy-weight steel or nothing at the By The Way. The steel shovel and I weighed the same. Centuries from now, when they do an archeological dig on that old farm, I'm convinced that shovel will still be there. An ancient farm tool still intact.

Levelling the chop out to the edges of the walls would continue until I was on my knees because there was too little room at the top to stand upright. The unwritten farmer's kid code meant I couldn't come out before it was time! Finally, I would stick the shovel up through the hole, chop still pouring in, as a last desperate signal to those idly standing around that it was time to turn the stupid auger off.

Most evenings, my chores included walking out to the pasture, about a quarter mile away, and chasing the Jersey cows back to the farm and into the barn for milking. Like trained animals, they were enticed by being fed grain and hay every night as their reward for giving up their milk. After countless trips, they learned the routine and were often waiting for me at the gate. I didn't do a lot of cow milking, but when I did, I would have to balance on a three-legged stool while the cow's tail slapped me on the side of the head, swatting flies. The real trick was holding the pail between my legs. It had to be at the perfect angle to have space to shoot the milk into while maintaining control and keeping the pail away from the cow's feet. I never perfected the art of cow milking. I seemed to always pick the one cow that would step in the half-filled pail of milk. I didn't take real kindly to milking cows and made a point of not getting very good at it. I hereby posthumously nominate the fellow who invented milking machines for a Nobel Prize for emancipating child labour!

If you wanted a dairy farm that sold milk, then Holsteins were the cows of choice. If you simply wanted milk to consume in the kitchen, to feed the pigs, and to sell the cream, then Jersey cows were the best. We had Jerseys. The milk from the cows had three purposes:

1) To make cream for sale. The milk would be poured into

the cream separator, aptly named for the process of separating the cream from the milk through centrifugal force. Witnessing the cream come out one spout while milk came out the other was always a technical marvel to me and still is.

2) To consume. We would pour the un-homogenized, un-pasteurized, un-chilled milk into a jar for eating cereal and cooking.

3) To feed the pigs, which was the bulk of the milk. Feeding the milk to the pigs was not as much fun as separating the milk. It had the same appeal as spreading chop, albeit without the itch and burial potential.

The two ten-gallon pails of milk I had to carry from the barn to the pig shed every night weighed more than I did. It remains a mystery to me how milk turns into lead once it's poured into a pail. I was also short and the top of the pails came up past my knees. The best I could do was to raise the pails up about six inches and then walk a few feet at a time before my arms would weaken, causing the bottom of the pail to smash and skin my ankles. I tried everything from holding one pail at a time between my legs to running with the pails to maximize the distance travelled before dropping the pail. If I had to stop nine times on the way over, all of a hundred yards long, or lessen the load by pouring some on the ground, then so be it. Some nights, the pigs just went to sleep hungry.

Like the song says, "Christmas is a Wonderful Time of

the Year." Sounds a bit trite, but as a small kid on a farm, it was a magical time. I absolutely loved Christmas.

The first sign that it was coming for real was in early December. On a Saturday shopping trip to town, and hopefully a movie, we would stop at a tree lot to buy the Christmas tree, usually a fir. We'd all get out of the car and tag along with Dad and Mom as they walked every aisle and looked at every tree. Dad would pick one out, untie it, shake off the snow, and let the branches unfurl. He would then twirl it around so Mom could see all sides. It had to be perfect. "What do you think of this one, Mary?" he would ask. Mom would point out the tree's flaws and we'd all move on. To me, every tree looked good enough. How could this take so long? At age six I was already showing signs of future impatience. Finally, the best tree would be put in the car trunk. It was always too long, so the bottom end went in first, leaving the top end sticking out behind. The trunk lid would be secured with binder twine for the trip home.

Decorating the tree in our house was probably the same as millions of others around the world, but to us it was a special occasion. First things first, Dad had to clamp it into the triangle tree stand, but not without first cutting the bottom off to exactly the right height and level to better soak up water in the tray. Then came the trimming of the branches. It never failed that once the tree got home it seemed to have altered its shape for the worse. A gaping hole here or an uneven branch there was not to be tolerated. With Mom supervising, Dad would drill a hole in the gap and then jam in a branch cut from the back. The back side, of course, would face the wall. Finally, we had our perfect tree, although pictures from the family archives seem to show otherwise.

Decorating the tree was next and that's where Irv, Stuart, Jean, and I joined in to help. First up was to hang the three strings of lights, some farther in and some farther out for a fuller effect. Next, we'd hang the ornaments. As each one was brought out of the box, memories of Christmas past would return. Then came the tinsel, brand new and neatly hanging inside several cardboard packages. Then came the angel hair, which looked like bits of white cotton candy that we pulled slightly apart and placed in front of a bulb to create a warm glow. Fortunately, the angel hair was fireproof; unfortunately, I think it was made of asbestos. Angel hair was certainly a misnomer. Finally, an angel ornament was placed on top and the tree was done. Everyone would then eagerly anticipate plugging in the tree lights. Every year, only one string would light up. The next step was like a game. Who would be the first to find the single burned out or loose bulb, or harder yet, several bulbs. It could only be solved through the process of elimination, one bulb at a time. When someone hit pay dirt, the whole tree would light up. Now Christmas could start for real.

Christmas was really all about the presents. Jesus could have returned and come to our very house that night, but it was Santa who we *really* wanted. Religion can wait when you're a kid! After years of giving homemade gifts to Mom and Dad (like a letter holder made of paper plates with Merry Xmas scrawled in crayon), we each got five dollars to buy them a *real* present, usually at the local hardware store.

Although not wealthy by any means, my parents were able to afford some luxuries. Mom and Dad were always generous with us at Christmas. Not so much in quantity, but in quality. We were often the first to get the newest toy, like an electric race car set on a circle-eight track.

Arranging for presents to arrive on time (other than the ones from Santa) took some careful planning on Mom's part. They had to be ordered from Sears or Eatons and shipped by bus or train from the east to our little prairie hamlet of Throne, way out west. Weeks before, Mom would ask what we'd like for Christmas. I would browse through the catalogues until I picked something out, like a Roy Rogers gun and holster set, a chemistry set, or, of all things, a guitar. Mom would then hold the catalogue open with one hand and start filling out the order sheet with the other. So much for the element of surprise. It didn't really matter anyway. Given the small size of our house, there were few hiding spots for presents, as I discovered once when searching in their closet and finding a BB gun. As thrilled as I was that I was getting the BB gun, I was disappointed in myself for taking away my own surprise. I never went looking again.

I slept upstairs, as did Stuart and Irv while he was at home. On the morning of Christmas Day, we would be up well before dawn and come down the stairs. Jeannie's room was downstairs beside Mom and Dad's room, so I'd quickly go in to wake her up. With her bright eyes and cute smile, she'd jump out of bed to join in the excitement. I have forever etched in my memory the sights we saw when we walked into the living room each year. It was a miniature version of an FAO Schwartz toy store, only with a million less items. We would turn the tree lights on and open our stockings, filled mostly with candies and oranges while waiting for Mom and Dad to get up.

Dad insisted that we all eat breakfast before opening presents. He may as well have asked me to stop peeing when only half done. It was nearly impossible. Cereal and milk was all I needed; even toast would delay things too long. As soon as the last bite was downed, we kids would head to the living room and take our pre-picked out spot on the floor. A blizzard of tissue paper would fill the living room as presents were opened with thanks quickly voiced before moving on to the next one. In no time, everything was opened and, as always, everybody was happy.

Mom would then get up to put the turkey on and I swear our turkey was in the oven by nine o'clock to be ready in time for supper at six. Nine hours! Today, turkeys are fully grown in less than nine hours. Somewhere along the way, ovens must have gotten a lot hotter or clocks have gotten a lot faster. Nowadays, two to three hours and the turkey is done. I can't figure it out.

Learning to drive a tractor is a rite of passage for a farm kid. No driver's licence required, even at the age of ten. If you don't kill yourself, or more importantly anyone else, you're qualified to drive a tractor. Since I couldn't lift anything over twenty pounds, driving a tractor was a godsend. I have been a fan of mechanical devices ever since.

The government gave the farmers a break on the cost of gasoline used for farming, and only for farming. It was not for use in cars and trucks while driving on the highways. In order to distinguish the cheap, tax-free gas from the full price, taxed gas, it was coloured purple. Not surprisingly, the government didn't trust the farmers! The local police even did random highway checkstops to test a car's gas tank. With both a sense of importance and embarrassment, the local RCMP would open the gas cap, insert a glass syringe, squeeze the rubber ball at the top, and collect a sample. As little kids in the backseat, we were much more concerned about being late for the movie than Dad going to jail. Then, like a CSI detective at a bloody crime scene, the policeman would hold it up to the light to see what colour it was. Purple got you a steep fine, even if you feigned surprise and blamed the hired man for filling the car with the wrong gas.

On our farm, the large gas tank sat atop a ten-foot stand that had a horizontal plank on it for "the gas man" to stand on when filling the tank. I considered this the basecamp of my own Mount Everest. This was where I would jump up and grab the input cap of the steel tank and pull myself up to the top. Once I had scaled the peak, I would straddle my short legs, sticking straight out sideways, and look around. I was awed by what I saw from up there in the clouds. I could see across the whole yard. And I did it all without oxygen, pitons, or safety ropes. Like any mountain climb, descending was tougher and riskier. When sliding blindly down the tank's side on my back, I hoped to land on the plank and not be carried over into the abyss and sure death. To a little boy, the ten feet might as well have been a thousand.

The stand had stood in place for years, but eventually needed replacing. Dad and the hired man eventually built a new gas stand. It took several weeks as they only worked on it when they had spare time. The new one was also ten feet high and had two crossbeams like giant Xs at each end to keep it stable. Dad never said so, but there was a sense of pride when the stand was finished and the shining silver gas tank was hoisted into its resting place and then filled to the top with purple gas. All ready for the upcoming harvest season.

Now, filling up a tractor on a farm is not rocket science. You drive up to the stand, take off the gas cap, grab the hose nozzle, and fill 'er up with the colour purple. Unless, of course, you're a fourteen-year-old kid who gets rattled easily.

I was driving the John Deere tractor down the lane and across the yard at full speed. There stood the Trojan Horse, our new wooden gas stand with the 500 gallon steel tank glistening in the sun. But I had a dilemma. There were two caps: one for gas and one for water, and I didn't know which cap was which. It was quite important that I get it right. "Is it the one on the front or the one in the middle? Do I come in straight or sideways?" I asked myself. My indecision had drastic results. The tractor smashed into the left front corner of the stand, the one built to last forever. Forever, as it turned out, was less than two days. The Trojan Horse was leaning badly. I didn't bother to fill up the tank while I was there. I thought it best not to move anything in case it only made matters worse. There was enough propellant in the tank hanging precariously on the edge to send both the tractor and me to the moon several years ahead of Apollo 11.

Had there been a subsequent grand jury inquiry, they would have concluded that, besides being inept and indecisive, I was also driving too fast. I still have a psychological block of the conversation with my father afterwards, but I can vaguely recall the gist of it.

"Where's the tractor?" Dad asked.

"Over by the gas tank," I squeaked.

"The gas tank, why?"

"I hit the tank stand."

Sometimes it's best to know when to stop talking if you want to stay healthy. I stopped talking.

Today, I pride myself on my culinary skills. Nothing fancy, but certainly passable. My first foray into cooking, though, had a somewhat auspicious start. It was a summer Sunday and for some reason everyone was going away for the day, leaving me at home and in charge. "In charge" was only a figure of speech, of course, for at only twelve years old I wasn't really in charge of anything. My job description was simple enough. Try not to burn the place down or get myself killed. I did have one specific order to comply with: put the chicken in the oven so it would be ready for dinner upon everyone's return. Mom's instructions were short and precise.

"Dougie," she said, "take the chicken out of the fridge at four-thirty, place it in the oven, turn the oven on bake, and set it at 350 degrees. It's already in the pan and ready to go."

"Okay," I replied.

"Don't forget! Four-thirty!"

"I know, Mom, don't worry. I can handle it." I was annoyed at her implied lack of trust.

All afternoon I played outside, but kept going back into the house every so often to check the time. If I missed the deadline, I would not survive the consequences. Finally, the time came and I put the chicken in the oven.

"Okay, in the oven. Turn the dial to bake. Set the

temperature to three hundred fifty." This was the first time I had ever operated the oven. A small red light appeared. The power was on and the chicken was baking. Easy. What was she so worried about? I wondered.

After playing outside for, I would guess a half an hour, I thought I better check on *my* chicken. The red light was off! I logically and anxiously deduced that no red light meant the oven was off. Now what? I fiddled with the temperature dial and to my delight the red light came on. With a sigh of relief that I had "fixed the oven," I headed back out to play. About fifteen minutes later, I went back in. The stupid oven had shut off again! Again, I adjusted the temperature up and again got results. The red light and the oven were back on. We were back in the cooking business.

My check-and-fix routine repeated itself every fifteen minutes. By the time six o'clock came around, I had the oven hot enough to smelt iron ore. I lifted the roasting pan lid and crapped my pants! The chicken wasn't just done, it was DONE! I had just pulled a culinary first of transforming a farm-raised, free-range chicken into crispy Peking Duck. All that remained was black skin and bones. I took it out, turned off the oven, and waited for my execution.

Being a kid and, as some might say, not always thinking clearly, I failed to grasp the purpose of the red light. It indicated that the oven had reached the proper temperature, not that it had gone off. Well, it would have been nice if someone had told me this! What am I? A chef?

Words don't exist that adequately describe the family's reaction when they arrived home. Suffice to say, we ate mostly vegetables for dinner that night and my cooking career was put on permanent hold.

Finding somewhere to cool off in the hot summer sun on the prairies required resourcefulness and intelligence, which at times I came up a bit short on. In fairness, though, it wasn't like there were a whole lot of choices of where to swim.

My "Olympic pool" was a small rectangular dugout at the bottom of a hill about a quarter mile from the farm. It was called a dugout for a reason. Six feet deep in the centre and about fifteen by thirty feet on the sides, it was dug out to catch the rain and spring runoff. The only similarity it had to a real pool was its drowning capability. Each end consisted of ten feet of gradual slope of pure muck, urine, and manure, where the cattle had stood knee-deep for their daily drink of alkali-polluted water. Peeing in it actually improved the water quality. It was my very own Three Mile Island.

At ten to twelve years old, wearing a bathing suit no bigger than a thong and carrying a towel, I would wander down the hill to cool off. *Cooling off* was my objective, given I didn't know how to swim. Upon arrival at *the pool,* a welcoming party of a million mosquitoes hovered an inch above the surface ready to suck every drop of blood out of any living thing that dared enter. If one could document the degree of risk taken and the liberty given farm children back then, one could make a compelling case study for a Master's Degree in Child Care. After struggling through near-quicksand, I'd plunge feet first into the water. I kept only my head out of the water in order to avoid the mosquitoes. Now cooled off and getting bored, I would try to take a step, but would sink into the mud. Not many people get the chance to be bored while trying not to drown at the same time. Thirty minutes later, the next challenge was getting out.

Exiting meant walking through the same deep muck that fifty cows had trod and defecated in only hours before and exposing myself to the gauntlet of mosquitoes that had waited patiently, knowing that sooner or later this kid had to come out of the water. They were the smartest mosquitoes on the prairies. Once out, I would dip my muddy legs back into the water until I could see some resemblance of skin, all the while slapping at hundreds of mosquitoes that had already found the buffet on my face, arms, and back, and then trek back to the farm for a shower of ice-cold water from the garden hose.

I eventually learned to swim in that old dugout, diving in from one side and letting sheer momentum and a couple of arm flails take me to the other side, then reversing the routine. Thankfully, I did learn to swim because it may have been days before I was found otherwise.

My favourite movies were always Westerns. The

cowboys were my heroes. Television only came to our house when I was about fourteen, but the movies and comic books had always kept me fully supplied with cowboy heroes to imitate and worship: Alan Ladd, Audie Murphy, Gary Cooper, Jimmy Stewart, Roy Rogers, Gene Autry, The Lone Ranger, Rex Allen, among others.

After watching a Western at the Avalon, and heading over to the Royal Crown, I would transform into a Greek centaur. From the waist up, I was the cowboy star, wearing a brown buckskin jacket; from the hips down, I was the horse. I would gallop down the sidewalk slapping my bum as if whipping my horse to full speed to catch the bad guys or shoot the Indians. I was The Lone Ranger *and* Silver all rolled into one. We were connected at the hip.

Our ranch was a perfect setting for the Old West and for playing out our fantasies. One day I would be the cowboy and the next day the cavalry. Our corral was the OK Corral, the barn was the livery stable, and the Hereford cows were the Texas Longhorns. The haystacks were the deep canyons that served as perfect hiding places for the bad guys. With toy western pistols, holsters and all, I could stand up to anybody, anytime. I was always the good guy.

Long before political correctness reared its ugly head, we would also dress up as Cheyenne or Apache Indians. This got boring pretty fast, so Stuart and I would shoot our arrows straight up in the air just to see how high they would go. Trouble was, we'd lose sight of them in the sun and then have no idea where they'd come down, or when. We'd cover our heads with our arms and hold our breath and wait, and wait, for a thud, hopefully. Time passes so slowly when you're awaiting death by arrow to the head. Thankfully, they never came straight down.

Of course, living on a real ranch meant that we actually did real cowboy work. I was maybe thirteen when Stuart and I were given orders to check on the herd of cattle grazing about a mile from the ranch. We would need to ride west on the gravel road for a half mile, then ride another half mile through an empty field to the far pasture.

"Why not wear my gun and holster?" I thought. "I'll tie a string on each pistol to make sure that if they fall out of the holster, I won't lose them. Brilliant! But how long to make the string? Three inches would be too short to 'grab for leather' quickly. Three feet should do it." I cut each piece of old binder twine to identical lengths and then tied one end to the top of the holster and the other to the handle of the pistol.

As often is the case, the first idea is brilliant, while the second idea is one too many.

We rode side by side, Stuart and I, two cowboys going to check the herd. Stuart rode Buck, the buckskin gelding, and I rode the chestnut mare Tinkerbell. (I called her "Champ.") We arrived at the pasture, counted the cows, and checked them over. Our work done, we headed home.

I started Champ off at a slow gallop when instantly both

pistols fell out of their holsters. The strings did their job, but far too well. Three feet of string turned out to be the perfect distance from the holster to Champ's underbelly. With each gallop the two pistols flew straight out at waist-high level on each side, and then, in perfect 4/4 time, dropped back down and hit the horse in the belly. My six shooters were far more effective than any whip or spurs. Champ bolted at full speed, heading straight for the ranch. I stood in the saddle and pulled on the reins, but Champ weighed a half a ton and I weighed less than the saddle.

Try as I might, I could not pull the pistols up and place them back in the holster. Each time they bounced up, I tried to grab one in mid-air, but they were always an inch out of reach. A couple seconds later and they were back up and I would try again. Snatching a fly in midair was easier. Staying in the saddle quickly became an even higher priority than grabbing the guns. Falling off at thirty miles an hour would create a whole different set of problems.

Champ ran across the field and then down the hard gravel road. The noise of the hooves hitting the hard ground almost made me let go out of pure fright. As long as I stayed in the saddle, I felt I had a chance of surviving. All of this begs the question: Where was Stuart while all this was happening? If it had been the movies, he would have ridden up beside me at full gallop so I could leap from my horse onto his. But Stuart was nowhere to be seen and I dared not try looking backwards for fear of falling off.

The next hurdle in my race to doom was the main gate to the ranch, off to the right and coming up fast. I wondered if Champ would make the turn. She did! As if there was a wall only she could see, she took a sharp right hand turn at full speed without the slightest pause. I barely managed to hang on by leaning far to my right side. She continued galloping down the lane towards the corral, where the end was in sight. One way or the other! She stopped dead in front of the corral gate. Like a human cannonball, I was ejected out of the saddle and flew perfectly horizontal over her head, with two guns following exactly three feet behind like drone missiles. About ten feet out, Newton's law took over and I fell to the ground in a heap. It was a miracle that the pistols missed my head and didn't fracture my skull. My romanticized trail ride of singing in the saddle with guns on my hip and spurs a-jingling came to an unceremonious end, in a heap on the ground. I was scratched up and my pride hurt, but who said being a cowboy star was going to be easy?

Only then did Stuart and Buck come sauntering down the lane.

Inga and Neils Jensen were Danes who wanted to immigrate to Canada to start a new life. Mom and Dad offered to hire Neils to work on our farm as "the hired man." They packed up what little they had into a couple of suitcases and took a ship to Canada, and the train to Coronation. They spoke not a word of English, so the trip must have been frightful for them.

They were to live in the little house across the yard from our "little house on the prairie." It was the original farmhouse that my grandpa had built in the 1900s and, although it had electricity, it had no running water and no indoor plumbing. But, over the next year, a wonderful transformation took place as they made it *their* home. They fixed up the house and planted beautiful flower and vegetable gardens.

I vividly recall the first morning after they arrived. They were invited over to our house for breakfast and, as it turned out, their first lesson in English. Pointing to a Corn Flakes box, the one with the rooster and a cob of corn, Dad said, "corn." After a couple of attempts, including smiles and grins back and forth, they managed to say the word "corn." How ironic. One of the first things the Mayflower pilgrims learned was corn and there we were teaching the same word to immigrants on their first day. It was déjà vu 1690! Many years later, Neils and Inga explained to us how they were shocked that we even ate corn. Where they came from corn was only fed to farm animals.

Mom sometimes invited Inga over to the house for coffee. More than once, Inga would reach into her apron pocket and realize that she forgot her cigarettes, Buckingham Plain (no filter). Jean and I would be instructed to go over to Inga's house and fetch the cigarettes for her. It never crossed our minds that Inga would notice a missing cigarette or two. When the FDA eventually banned the worst cigarettes, Buckingham Plain must have been at the top of the list. They were strong enough to knock a bull to its knees. As I learned many years later as a smoker, if there is one thing a smoker instinctively knows, it's whether the pack is missing even one cigarette. Inga never squealed, likely choosing job security over accusing the boss's kids of being crooks.

To say that smoking was our first vice is technically wrong. Stealing the cigarettes qualified as grand larceny, so in comparison, smoking was a minor offence. Getting a few wooden matches out of our cupboard without being spotted was no easy task either. We were smart enough to know that asking for matches, having just brought over Inga's Buckinghams, was akin to a guy with a balaclava over his head asking where the bank was.

The next decision was where to commit our next criminal act. With one hiding the cigarette and the other the matches, it was a scene right out of Prohibition. We searched for the best Speakeasy. We chose a different place each time, including the hopper of the combine or underneath the old threshing machine. The best place, we concluded, was the empty granary. We had a total disregard for the foot of dry grain and dust residing in the bottom just waiting to explode with even the slightest spark. On the inflammatory scale of 1 to 10, it was a 10. We may as well been sitting on a pail of gasoline. It's a wonder we never burned the whole farm down.

I don't recall whether it was Jean or I who took the first

step on the path of becoming a potential hardened criminal, but no matter. The reaction was the same as we took our first puff. The initial proud feeling that we were getting away with something quickly gave way to coughing and choking and butting out the cigarette on the wall. Where were filtered cigarettes when we needed them?

Jean never took much to cattle or farming. Her only experience was joining the local 4-H Beef Club for one year, along with Stuart and me. A large multi-national organization, 4-H teaches rural children about feeding and raising beef steers for the market. I never understood why it was called the 4-H. The Hs stood for head, heart, hands, and health; none of which had anything to do with cattle. But when Jean told Dad she wanted to join, I knew it was for the wrong reason. "She just wants to meet boys," I argued at the supper table. No one listened or cared. I also knew that Stuart and I would be the ones caring for Jean's calf over the next eight months before the sale. We would be the ones dragged on our stomachs through the manure and dirt in the corral trying to halter-break her calf. We would be the ones feeding the steer twice a day and washing and grooming it when it came time for the show and sale ("Achievement Day" in 4-H vernacular). Many 4-H-ers were known to cry when they sold the steer they had personally raised and cared for. Not Jean. When it came time for the big show, Jean asked, "Which calf is mine?" The prosecution rested its case!

Every second summer in the 1950s, save for maybe one or two, we would drive to Campbell River, British Columbia, to visit our grandparents, Pop and Gran. One year, they came to Alberta by train, but all the other times we headed west to see them. It was two days there, a week of visiting, and two days back.

The process never varied. Mom would wash, iron, and pack our clothes the night before, and we kids would lie wide awake most of the night, too excited to sleep. In the morning, we'd all pile in the Buick. Jean would sit in the front seat with Mom and Dad, while we three boys, two later on, would be in the back, bugging each other. Dad would back the car out of the garage, put it in first gear, and begin to drive up the lane. We were on our way, or so we thought. Halfway up the lane, Dad would stop the car, take it out of gear, turn around, lean on the seat, and shake his finger at us.

"If you kids don't stop fighting right now, we're stopping right here and not going!"

One hundred yards into our eight hundred-mile trip and we were already at a dead stop. At this pace, it would take a year just to get to the main highway. We'd clam up and look at our feet. No one dared look up for fear of being singled out. The first couple of trips we took his threat seriously, but we soon figured out it was a veiled threat at best. There was no way we weren't going when the car was packed and the trip had been planned for weeks.

Finally, we were off!

If it was hot, and often it was, we'd drive with all the windows down. Air conditioning for cars didn't exist back then. We in the back couldn't hear anything with the noise of the gushing wind.

The route was always the same, except for one time. To Calgary and then straight west over the mountains. There was no Rogers Pass then, so we had to take the "Big Bend" route, swinging way north in the interior of BC and then back down again. On each trip, we would ask Dad to stop and let us read the historical signs beside the highway. "We have to make a mile," he'd say, "but we'll stop on the way back." But it was the same going home: no stopping to read signs. We did our best to read the signs at sixty mph, picking out the odd word and filling in the spaces on our own. Was that three or thirty people who died building the railroad? Or maybe it was three hundred?

We really enjoyed watching for the little wooden arrows on top of posts pointing towards particularly high mountain peaks with their height painted on the board. Those we could read, even at warp speed, and always anxiously looked forward to the next one that might show a mountain higher than any before. It's a shame these signs are all gone now. Why some government bureaucrat decided to take them down is beyond me. We should be proud of our mountains.

Lunch meant a rolling stop at a little restaurant. Why Dad even bothered to shut off the car is a wonder. The stopover process was "dumbed down" to ensure nothing could go awry and hold up the trip: get out of the car, pee, sit, eat, pee again, get back in the car. If there had been take-out windows back then, we would never have stopped. We were cheap kids to take on a trip—always cheeseburgers and fries, a Coke or chocolate milkshake. I remember Dad's favourite milkshake was strawberry. Funny what we remember as kids. On the farm, one learns to eat quickly lest there were not enough seconds for all. This skill came in quite handy when travelling, given we had to eat fast to "make a mile."

As dusk approached, the search for a motel would begin with all eyes looking out all windows to find one. Stuart and Irv would look out their side windows, while I would stand up in the middle and hold onto the back of the front seat, trying to look ahead. This was made more difficult because Jean was standing up in the front holding onto the dash or the rearview mirror.

There was no Internet to search, so it was trial and error for all travellers. Around the bend, approaching a small town, we would see some neon lights in the distance. The names were simple but telling: "The Shady Rest," "The Cedar Inn," "The Pine Cabins," and "The Last Stop." I'm convinced there were three "Last Stop" motels in the same town.

The first thing we looked for was a "Vacancy" sign, or worse, a "NO Vacancy" sign. There are things in life that were better before technology ran amuck. If I run for political office, my election platform will include bringing back vacancy signs.

If there was motel competition, and usually there was, then the real attractions flashed in a neon colour different than the name. Better for all to see! Pool, or better yet, Heated Pool; TV, and later, Coloured TV; Phones! Yes, phones were even a big seller. We would get excited, but none of these things mattered in Mom and Dad's selection criteria. They wanted a kitchenette and it had to be clean. Funny how the cleanest motels never had a pool or a TV.

If there was a vacancy sign, and the motel looked decent, we would stop and Mom would go in and check it out. If she came back flailing her arms like a flagman on an aircraft carrier, then that was the signal to go park the car. Flailing arms meant relief all around. Hours and hours of driving had mercifully come to an end, at least for the day. We had just hit the mother lode. If she didn't flail her arms, she'd simply jump back into the car and we'd be off to continue the search.

It was now bail out of the car time and haul in what we needed for the night, including sleeping bags and the green Coleman stove, complete with a mini canister of fuel. I still wonder what that fuel was. After a few tries of pumping and lighting, and muttering vulgarities under her breath, Mom would get the stove lit and dinner cooking: hamburgers, pork chops, or chicken; fried potatoes and a boiled vegetable. Presto, we had a meal Joe's Diner could not have served up any better.

The next morning, while still dark, they woke us to

get washed and dressed. After bacon and eggs, fried on the Coleman (God bless our Coleman stove), the race renewed and we were off at first light. "Got to make time. Need to catch the ferry in time for lunch," was the battle cry on the second day.

When it comes to car design, I'm glad new technology showed up when it did. Driving over mountain passes in the 1950s and early '60s meant overheated radiators. Today, I don't even know if my SUV has a radiator, or if I'd even be able to find the radiator cap. Despite our hell-bent schedule, our car couldn't care less. It had its own schedule. When it boiled over, you pulled over. Up went the hood and then we all waited, until the steel radiator cap cooled enough to unscrew. Every five minutes or so, with his hand wrapped in a towel or a jacket, Dad would slowly reach over and try the cap. A little twist, a little air vent, and the steam would come roaring out like Ol' Faithful. It was always too soon. Dad would leap back, holding his almost-burned hand, cuss a bit, and the wait would continue. Nobody dared suggest he had tried too soon! But the quicker he got it off, or at least depressurized, the sooner it cooled and could be refilled and we'd be on our way. In about an hour, he could get the cap off and refill the radiator with cold water, which was usually available, fortunately, in a small running steam alongside the road. After locating the radiator cap that had been thrown about twenty feet away because it was still too hot to hold, Dad would screw the cap back on and the Gillards were off again.

Despite stops for radiators boiling over, getting stuck behind cars pulling trailers, and repeatedly stopping for pee breaks, we still managed to catch the ferry over to Vancouver Island in time for lunch. This was one of my favourite memories. In those days, the national rail company owned the ferries and they actually had dining service on the two-hour crossing. White table clothes, silverware, and fine china were something really special to us kids. We had never seen such fanciness before. Mom's Coleman food was good, but this was heaven. To kids from a farm, it didn't get better than this. Salmon all around, fresh out of the ocean! I'm convinced though that we kids got Captain Highliner and not the real stuff. But we didn't know any better.

After a week with Pop and Gran, it was time to start the process in reverse. Same missed historical signs, same motels, same meals. It may have been repetitive, and at times boring, but there was no better time for us than when we took our summer holiday by car.

Only once did we drive in the wintertime to spend Christmas with Pop and Gran. It was a disaster and never attempted again. Forget the radiator boiling over. Now we had to "chain up the tires" to climb the high passes on ice and snow-covered roads. We had no idea just how stressed Dad must have been driving under such tough conditions, but we always felt safe in our large and invincible car with Dad behind the wheel. But the inevitable happened. On a steep uphill climb on the Malahat Pass, just outside Victoria, a car came at us sliding on the ice sideways down the hill. We could all see it coming, but could only wait until he hit us head on. Both cars were totaled. Jean hit her nose on the rearview mirror, but otherwise we were all fine, despite not wearing seatbelts. A nice fellow who was driving behind us pulled over and offered to put us up at his home with his family in the city for the night. In the end, we took The Canadian train home to Calgary, where Dad bought a '52 Buick, and then drove it and us back to the farm. It was the only time we took a winter holiday.

The vacation I most looked forward to was going to the Calgary Stampede. As ranchers, Mom and Dad were keen rodeo fans (Dad actually competed in calf roping at local amateur rodeos). At least five times that I can remember, we drove to Calgary to attend the world famous Greatest Outdoor Show on Earth. Dressed in my best western wear of boots, jeans, and a new snap shirt, I was in my element. I was a real cowboy going to a real cowboy show. I loved it all: the Brahma bull, saddle bronc, and bareback riding events, as well as calf roping and steer wrestling. Jim Shoulders, Marty Wood, and Casey Tibbs were my rodeo heroes back then.

In the evenings, we would attend the chuckwagon races. Chuckwagon racing involved a team of four thoroughbred horses pulling a wooden wagon (like the chuck or cook wagons on the cattle trails in the 1800s) in a figure eight around two barrels set up in the infield. After circling the bottom barrel, they all hit the track at once and raced around a half-mile track, along with four outriders each, to the finish line. With four teams in a race, plus outriders, there were over thirty horses on the track at one time. It was an exciting, and very dangerous, event to watch. It was called the "Half Mile of Hell" for a reason. Major accidents were frequent, and sometimes fatal.

When we couldn't attend the real thing, I would turn on my transistor radio (with a brown leather case and six-inch antennae) and listen to Eric Bishop, the "Eye in the Sky." With my little red wagon at the ready and two metal cream cans in the middle of the dirt yard, I'd position myself in a standing start. I was the Merle Anderson rig on barrel #1. "And they're off for heat number eight!" the track announcer would call. In an instant, I'd have that red wagon flying in a circle eight around the cream cans. "Down the stretch they come!" I'd hear, matching them stride for stride to the finish line, always winning by a nose. Oh, how simple a life it was back then.

People who say they have no regrets are not being truthful. Everyone has at least one.

One of mine is that I never purchased land in the country and had my own ranch. It wasn't that I didn't have the means to acquire it. I even made an offer once on a quarter-section in the Alberta foothills, but I was always conservative when it came to real estate. My memories of growing up on the By The Way Ranch invoke romanticism and pleasant nostalgia that never leave me. To this day, I rarely miss attending the rodeo at the Calgary Stampede and watching the young cowboys walk in the footsteps of my childhood cowboy heroes. Like a meandering river that charts its own course, such is the same with life. Not all things happen as planned or hoped. The good news though is I had a ranch experience as a child and young adult that few have ever had.

CHAPTER 8
Sports

Next to speech and lack of creative skills, sports skills may have been my third greatest deficiency. I was more Mr. Bean than Mr. Jordan. I didn't even know where to put a jockstrap, much less own one. I tried one on once, but couldn't decide which end pointed up. I liked sports and tried everything: basketball (too short), jockey (too tall), fastball (too scared), football (too small). The failures were endless.

Jackie Mason, another famous comedian of the 1960s, once said something like, "I tried boxing once. I was knocked out in the first round. As I lay on the canvas listening to the referee count to ten, I said, 'Hey, I'll do the counting. You go get a doctor!'"

Mr. Baker, our Grade Six teacher, decided to teach us a little boxing. *Standing* in one corner was Curtis Bruggencate, five foot six and weighing 170 pounds of ready-to-rumble. *Cowering* in the other corner was I, four and a half feet and weighing 100 pounds of scared-out-of-my-wits. There were other distinguishing features between us. He shaved and I didn't. His voice had changed while I still spoke like a girl.

The only good news was I knew the consequences of coming out of the corner. But, in the interest of normalcy, out I came. My opponent was actually a nice guy and a good friend. We sparred a little, weaving and bobbing, occasionally touching gloves, as if we knew what we were doing. He took it easy on me until, in a single act of utter stupidity, I threw a quick left jab at his chin. The little wimp had gotten a shot in and the gloves were off, so to speak. Curtis was in a no-win situation with limited choices. He could hit me once and kill me, which would have been his preference, or take it on the chin literally and have everyone tease him. Fortunately, Mr. Baker stepped in and said, "Next up." I concurred.

Despite being the little guy, I didn't run away from trying sports, even given my zero success rate. I would always try. As far as I was concerned, I was normal; speech, size, and shape notwithstanding. Never thinking of what I had, or more importantly, what I didn't have, played a huge role in being able to achieve normalcy and success.

The regional track and field sports meet was coming up and it was try-out time for our school track team. The best would go on to compete in the regionals. Four of us tried out for three spots in the long jump. The other three guys made the team. Pole vaulting was out because I couldn't even lift one end of the pole. I ended up competing in the relay race. There were four teams: the fast guys, the two teams that thought they were fast, and my team. When we passed the baton on the second leg, the fast guys were already crossing the finish line. But we finished and that was all that mattered. It was time for an Orange Crush and a Cuban Lunch chocolate bar at the concession stand.

Noon hour pick-up softball games were fun, but only after the humiliating ritual of choosing teams. Each game started the same way. The two self-appointed best guys picked the two teams. First, they would toss the bat up vertically and one would grab it partway down the handle. Then, they would each take turns placing one hand above the other until they reached the top. The last full grip got first pick. It was all very scientific and done strictly by the rules.

"I'll take Tom," one captain said, followed by the other, "I'll take Brian." Next was Bobby and then Don, and on it went. Each time a player was called, he would walk to the baseline side of that team with a grin while the rest stood in a crowd, praying to not be last. The size of the unpicked and unwanted group shrunk painfully slowly. I was always last. Mercifully, they didn't say, "And last, I'll take Dougie." It wasn't necessary anyway. Everyone, including me, already knew the outcome.

Someday the inevitable will happen and I will leave this

world. At the pearly gates, St. Peter will ask, "So, Mr. Gillard, what did you do with your time down on Earth?" I'm not sure how he'll react when I say, "Well, sir, I spent my entire life trying to hit a little white ball into a four-inch hole." I can see him now, great tally book in hand, writing "nil" under the "Contribution to Society" section.

To my parents' credit, probably Mom more than Dad, they encouraged me to take up golfing. They didn't golf themselves, but somehow figured that I needed some kind of interest, and golf seemed like something I could do. So at twenty years old (very old in today's golf phenom terms), they bought me a starter set from the Woodward's department store. A full set consists of fourteen clubs, while the starter set had only seven clubs: a driver, a fairway wood, putter, wedge, and a nine, seven, and five iron. No matter, I now had a set of clubs, a red golf bag, and a keen desire to learn.

To say that I developed a passion for golfing is a gross understatement. Why I felt such a passion, I'm not sure. Besides being a great social sport, I finally found a sport that I could actually excel at. For once, I was not too small or too big or too slow. Sure, it helps to be strong and flexible, but eye-to-hand coordination and a consistent swing will put up lower scores than the big hitter who has no idea where the ball is going. It's also as competitive as you want it to be and I love the competition.

I eventually asked my future wife, Rosie, if she had ever golfed. To her credit, she answered honestly, with a firm "no."

(I had lied to her about skiing.) I knew that if I was to continue with my passion, I had to get her enthusiastic as well. If she didn't play all the time that would be fine (better, in fact), but I needed her to appreciate my addiction. Initially, she wasn't too keen to learn such a "silly game," but she was willing to try on those rare occasions when she wasn't working or taking her daughters somewhere. The day finally came when, while playing with friends, she hit the ball well and scored under 100. She was hooked. It was like unleashing a monster.

"I'm going to break ninety really soon," she said that night, while swinging a phantom club in the living room. I smiled. Breaking ninety would take a lot of practice and time. About two years later, she broke ninety at Pinebrook, our new home golf club. Her foursome was rooting for her and she was determined to complete the last hole before dark. I will always remember standing beside the green watching her make the putt for an eighty-nine, and then seeing her beautiful smile. She had achieved her goal and I couldn't have been happier for her.

What golf did for us more than anything was lead us to making several best friends, individually as well as couples. We would travel the world together, form gourmet dinner clubs, and attend numerous social functions. When just the two of us travelled, we would play golf along the way, hooking up with complete strangers. More often than not, when we arrived at the course for our booked tee time, the other two players would be men, not another couple. No matter. Rosie would step right up and show 'em what she had.

Playing golf together, as all couple golfers know, often tests the strength of the marriage. Every husband golfer I know has experienced their wife's wrath because they said the wrong thing at the wrong time, or said nothing when they should have said something. Unsolicited advice to a woman who is playing poorly is an absolute no-no, but men are slow learners, or masochists, or both.

We usually walk when we play, but when we share a golf cart together, it is the equivalent of "The Honeymooners." To play golf well takes a certain amount of concentration, which is impossible when I drive the cart. I get distracted at Rosie's comments to "turn here," "turn there," "start slowly," "slow down," "stop!" By halfway around, I just accept that my score will be my second worst of the year, beating only the other round I played earlier with Rosie.

Many courses have a rule that the cart is to be driven on the cart paths only, unless heading to your ball, in which case you turn off the path once you are approximately equal to the ball on the fairway. No one expects the turn to be absolutely precise, except Rosie. To her, this ninety-degree turn is a hard and fast rule, and it is as important as landing the Rover on Mars. She must have a carpenter's square in her head, for even an eighty-degree turn will result in, "Hugh, it's ninety degrees! That wasn't ninety degrees!"

For golfers, thousands of rounds of golf contain moments of potential greatness, utter frustration, laughs, high-fives, and taking the Lord's name in vain. I simply cannot imagine what my life would have been like without golf.

Many memorable golf instances stand out for me, including my good friend Ozzie throwing me out of a fast-moving golf cart. Going downhill on the famous Jasper Park #8 hole, Ozzie took an unannounced ninety-degree left turn and ejected me out the right side, without so much as touching the cart. I was lucky I didn't break my neck or spine. I had hit the ground approaching Mach One speed, then caught my spikes in the ground and flipped end over end into a sand trap. Somehow, I had managed to hold on to my golf club, a nine iron, which I then wielded over my head as I ran towards the cart to kill him. He was ducking down behind the cart, laughing so hard that I couldn't help but stop and laugh as well until I had tears in my eyes.

At the famous Banff golf course, I had hit my ball into a water hazard. I could see it about five feet out in the clear mountain water. I could reach it with a golf club if I leaned out far enough and someone held me by my other arm.

"I'll hold you, Gill," Ozzie said.

He grabbed my left arm with both his arms and braced himself. After this point, our versions of what happened vary greatly. Ozzie claims that instead of easing my way out,

I literally free-fell outwards, ending completely parallel to the water with my nose only two inches above it. He says he slipped and couldn't hold me. I was completely immersed in ice-cold water up to my waist. It was all my fault, apparently. Like a broken record, I was once again livid at him. I came out, dripping wet, <u>and</u> with no ball. I wanted to kill him, but couldn't as his laughter replaced my anger with laughter. Nobody ever made me laugh as hard or as often as Ozzie. It was impossible to stay mad at him.

The most memorable of all golf instances involved me only indirectly. For my fortieth birthday, Rosie organized a surprise golf weekend in Whitefish, Montana, with a few other couples. One of the couples was my sister, Jean, and her husband, Brian (Quig). Quig and I get along well now, but for many years our relationship, although cordial and respectful, was not in the category of bosom buddies. Maybe it was our competitive spirits that created the divide or my natural sibling protectionism of Jean. It was rare that we golfed in the same foursome, much less at the same course, or even on the same day. But, there we were, paired together in a foursome at the Columbia Falls Golf Club.

Our foursome was waiting at the seventeenth tee box as the group ahead of us played their second shot. Quig sat cross-legged on the grass, exposing his ivory white legs in a pair of shorts. (He rarely wore shorts and his skin didn't tan). I stayed in the cart out of the ninety-five-degree Fahrenheit heat without a breeze. Out of nowhere, some black spots splattered across the windshield. Then a few more. Then, like the skies opening up for a summer hailstorm, it rained down what I was sure was goose shit. The cart was covered! I looked over at Quig sitting on the grass. Brown crap was coming down in buckets and his head, shirt, shorts, and white legs were totally covered.

"What the hell!" he yelled.

I looked up, expecting to see a massive flock of geese, but there wasn't a bird in sight. After the hail of "whatever" ceased, I exited the cart. I saw something I had never seen before and will never see again. The golf cart and my brother-in-law were completely covered in shit. I was laughing so hard I could hardly stand up. The next foursome, including Jean and Rosie, then drove up behind us, stunned by the sight and smell.

"What kind of bird?" Jean asked, as if that mattered.

"Certainly not a robin," I answered.

The mystery of what rained down on us that day belongs in "Ripley's Believe It or Not." I am convinced that it was not a flock of geese, but a passenger plane that had accidentally (?) emptied its toilet. I've read that crap freezes at 30,000 feet, but I'm sure there's plenty of time for it to thaw out on the way down. The experts will argue to the contrary, but I know for a fact that no bird (or birds) exist that could drop that much crap at one time in one place, even if they knew it was Quig!

CHAPTER 9
Dating

Despite the odd setback, communication failures, teasing, stares, and the farm chores that I hated, I was a pretty well-adjusted kid. But, when I entered junior high school as a teenager, I was rather immature and way behind my peers physically, which compounded my unique differences. While the teen boys were aging and becoming men, I was aging but staying a boy. The only evidence that I was a teenager was my birth certificate. I was nowhere close to shaving yet and even my voice remained falsetto. What was really strange to me was that the guys all of a sudden were interested in girls and I had no idea why. They would snap the bras of the girls sitting in desks in front of them and laugh. I didn't even know they were called bras. I later learned that my developmental delays and cleft palate were connected. An even more unique syndrome: 1 in 10,000 as opposed to 1.4 in 1,000 for cleft palates.

At age fifteen, my friend Brian and I were at a movie at the Avalon. He had a crush on a girl named Carol and, as rumour had it, she and her friend June would be there that night. Carol was small and cute as a button with personality to burn. In fact, I had the biggest secret crush on her, which I harmlessly revealed to her at a reunion some fifty years later.

One row back and seated behind us, June and Carol constantly chatted and giggled back and forth. The news feature was over and the cartoon was just beginning when Brian got up and sat back beside Carol. I had no idea what to do, so I remained frozen in my seat, staring straight ahead. It was not long before there was a tap on my shoulder. I turned and saw Carol, smiling and patting the empty seat beside her, beckoning me to sit beside June. I was so pleased they asked, but inside I felt sheer terror. Not having a better idea, I moved back and sat in the seat beside June. I didn't blink for the rest of the movie. It wasn't a real date, but it was the first time I had "crossed to the wild side," and to my utter surprise, survived.

Wayne Benson was my good friend during the years between Grade Five and Grade Ten. He was taller than me, as almost everyone was, of blondish hair and typical, conservative farm boy traits. Wayne was sincere and loyal. In our mid-teen years, Keith, our mutual friend and a farm boy as well, had his own car, and the three of us would drive to and around Coronation, thinking we had grown up. In his car, we were free and independent! It can't get better than this, we thought.

At fifteen, a coming of age moment has become forever locked in my memory. As we walked up to the school for a high school dance one evening, Wayne motioned us over to a spot behind a tree. He opened his wallet and proudly took out a small object wrapped in gold foil.

"See what I got?" he said, beaming.

"Wow," Keith said, clearly impressed.

"Wow," I echoed. I had never seen such a thing before and had no clue what it was. Later, I learned that I had seen my first condom. As far as I know, the condom never came out of his wallet until after high school. On further thought, I heard that he later had several children, so maybe it's still in there.

At sixteen, I was starting to want to date girls. Not because of an overwhelming urge; I simply didn't like being behind my friends and not doing what they were doing. It also seemed like a lot of fun. Wanting to date and actually doing it, though, are two different things. I had gained a fair bit of confidence in a lot of things, except dating. All of my unique features—crooked teeth, funny talk, scars—still kept me self-conscious and shy with girls.

"Let's go to the dance at Brownfield Friday night," Ritchie said one day.

Ritchie's dad had a small farm just west of ours, even though they lived in the town of Veteran, five miles east. We had become best friends as little kids when his dad would drop him off to play. We would ride our bikes or walk to the Throne store and buy Cokes and candy, then return to our farm to play games and have the highest sugar rush possible. Once he got his driver's licence, he would come by in his dad's old red

International half-ton truck and pick me up to just drive around or go to his dad's farm. There was no doubt when Ritchie was driving by our farm because the line of dust he kicked up on the dirt road could be seen for miles. Dad would get so mad and always worry, legitimately, about how fast Ritchie drove.

"Sure, let's," I said.

I knew he'd be taking someone to the dance and I thought to myself, "It's time." Connie Lewis was a cute farm girl, a bit short and a little plump. I suppose someone somewhere has written a book on the human dating selection process because it seems people gravitate to those who have similar attractive standards, however measured. The handsome guy gets the gorgeous girl and, like magic, it all works from there. Given my unique features, there was no one of the opposite sex that fell into the same category as me. All the girls I knew back then were at least cute and a step up for me. Above all, Connie was nice and not dating anyone, if in fact she had ever dated.

So, I decided that Connie would be my first date ever. Maybe. The next day I managed to work up enough nerve to walk up to her at her locker and pose the most frightening question I had ever asked: "Would you like to go to the Brownfield dance this Friday night?"

Her answer came back in maybe three seconds, but to me enough time lapsed to triple my heart rate.

"Sure, that would be great," she replied with a smile.

I had never smiled much, if at all. But this time a huge

natural smile broke out. I was so happy. I was going on a real date!

I couldn't wait to tell Ritchie. As it turned out, he didn't have a date, which disappointed me, but he was supportive. On the way to Brownfield, a hamlet north of Coronation, we drove into the Lewis farm to pick up Connie. I approached the farmhouse door like any typical teenage kid on a first date. I was so nervous. Her mother came to the door to check out her daughter's first date; Connie followed closely behind in a pretty yellow dress. When we returned to the truck, Ritchie was all smiles.

After the dance, we drove back, first stopping to drop off Connie. I was nervous all over again as to how the evening would end. I'm not talking about sex, because neither of us knew what it was anyway. But still, some form of "goodnight" had to be said. When we came to a stop in the yard, Ritchie turned off the truck, turned out the lights, and, being a true friend, said, "Take your time."

We reached the front door of the house far too quickly. I hadn't yet figured out how I was going to end this. "Should I kiss her?" I wondered.

"Thanks, I really enjoyed it," I said.

She said the same and just like that it was over. No kiss, not even a hug. We were both too shy. Ritchie was stunned that I was back in the truck in under a minute. If it had been him, I'd have had to wait at least a half hour; his goodnights were much more time consuming.

All the way home, I couldn't stop feeling good about myself. Little did I know that my date with Connie would be the last for over ten years. I would be well into my mid-twenties before I dated again.

CHAPTER 10

The Big Move

In 1964, midway through Grade Eleven, a seismic shift took place in our lives. Mom and Dad had decided to sell the 3,000-acre ranch and move some 200 miles south to a sixty-acre place near Okotoks, a small town outside Calgary, Alberta. After years of hard work, they had decided to semi-retire while still relatively young. Mom was forty-one and Dad was fifty-three. Stuart and Irv were long gone, so just Jean and I would be affected.

Each year thousands of families relocate. It's traumatic for children as they seek new friends and establish new relationships. Although it was no different for us than for others, this did not lessen our anxieties. Compounding the issue was the fact that we moved in November, three months into the school year. Given that it was not a corporate or armed services move, Jean and I failed to see the need to move mid-year. "Why make it harder?" we asked. We thought their timing could have been more considerate of us teens.

If the bookies had set up a bet on who would handle the change the best, they would certainly have lost money.

Jean was a typical teenager in Grade Ten, putting more importance on girlfriends and dating than on school. Despite her great looks and outgoing personality, Jean was traumatized by the move, and it showed the first day she came home from the new school.

"I hate it," she said. I felt bad for her, but it wouldn't be long before she would make lifelong friends and be glad of the move.

I, on the other hand, came home that first day quite upbeat. All of the new classmates I had managed to meet were very nice. They were curious but respectful and friendly. They had already grown into respectful young adults. My first-day anxieties did not bear out, but then again, I had no great expectations either.

Age sixteen was no different from age fifteen. I was still short, underdeveloped, and socially immature. I still hadn't had a single minute of speech therapy or had my teeth straightened with braces. Three years earlier, I had had more oral surgery by the same Dr. Hitchen at the University of Alberta hospital, primarily to repair the cleft in the roof of my mouth and cover the inside vent to my nose. After the surgery, I remember asking the doctor why my jaw was so sore. He kindly responded with, "Well, that's because your jaws were kept wide open with a block for three hours." A neighbour told me afterwards that she thought the surgery had helped my speech, but if it did, it was marginal at best. The hole in my nose was definitely smaller but still existed. I could now drink from a water fountain.

To complete the nerd picture, I had gotten a hearing aid the year before. It was the type in a metal box that fit in my front pocket with a wire snaking up through my shirt to my left ear. At times I would adjust it in class without looking down and end up turning it up too high, causing a high-pitched squeal of feedback. One day, in frustration, I took it home, placed it in a drawer, and never wore it again.

Not long after starting at the new school, I attended my first Okotoks high school dance at the gym. I was very nervous. I didn't have any friends yet. Looking back, I'm proud of the fact that I never shrank away from the challenge of at least trying to be normal and doing what other kids do, even if almost every time the end result was less than satisfying.

Somewhere in the annals of high school dance history, a social dynamic developed that may still exist to this day. All the girls sat along the walls of both sides of the gym, while the boys, in a single mass of testosterone, stood at the back. They were like a pod of killer whales circling the minnows. The girls would face the dance floor, hoping some guy, but not the wrong guy, would ask them for a dance. The guys would use their built-in quality control mechanism to observe the girls. They'd sort the good looking, the average looking, and the not-so-good looking. All the guys wanted to upgrade without being turned down. Should I ask her? Or her?

Strategy was involved, too. It was crucial to see who was sitting in the seats at the far end of the row. No one would risk asking a girl in the middle to dance. If she said, "No thanks," then the walk of shame ensued. Imagine a teenage boy turning around and walking in front of all the previously passed girls, having just been rejected. More strategy was required for the "exit plan." If a guy walked within two girls of his target, only to hear her say "yes" to the guy walking ahead of him, an "exit plan" was desperately needed. Passing the now empty chair was no time to appear indecisive or acknowledge that the plan had changed! Should he ask the girl sitting next to the empty chair or not? Better to keep walking as if going to the washroom was the original plan. It was pure humiliation for everybody and the fact that anyone survived the culling ritual to dance another day was no small miracle.

As for me, my strategy was to wait until the song had already started and many girls had already headed to the dance floor. In this mass chaos of comings and goings, I'd approach someone still sitting, greatly diminishing the chance of being declined. A simple "yes" was all I needed to be "one of the boys." The good news was that I had become a pretty good dancer, having jived with Jean when we were kids. So, if the girl really liked to jive, my odds increased exponentially.

That same first night a drama ensued, like something out of the movie *American Graffiti*. I was Terry the Toad, played by Charles Martin Smith. He was the nerd, the virgin, wanting to be cool, but blowing every opportunity, and always trying to be just one of the guys. Wayne Rowland, a fellow classmate, was the exact opposite. He was John Milner: good looking, slicked back hair, cool, confident, idolized by the girls, and driving the hot car. Like all the other guys in my class, Wayne only knew me as the new kid in town, and a loner at that. Little did I know that Wayne and I would connect this night and become close friends for many years.

About halfway through the dance, a girl who lived south of town came in crying uncontrollably. She had passed a horrible fatal car accident on the gravel road about three miles south of town. The news spread around the dance quickly, with everyone wondering who was involved and who had died. So, what do young immature high school guys do? They jump in cars and drive out for a look at the wreck. On the way out of the school, Wayne saw me standing by myself with that "wanting to go" look and said, "Jump in with us if you want." John Milner had befriended Terry the Toad that night and, for the first time since moving to Okotoks, Terry the Toad felt like he belonged.

Wayne didn't make the offer because he wanted another friend, but his act of inclusion started a chain reaction that over time led me to becoming very close with a group of special guys of whom there were no equals. There was Wayne (Al), David (Ozzie), Wayne (Butch), Mike, Donnie (Mouse), and me (Gill). Family comes first, but this group of loyal friends run a very close second. "The Band of Brothers," as I affectionately call us (with apologies to Stephen Ambrose, who wrote the famous book), was my ticket to normalcy. Without my time with them, individually or as a group, I would never have progressed as much as I did, both socially and professionally.

Wayne was the first to extend his hand of friendship, but sadly, nearly fifty years later, he was the first of the gang to pass away. I spoke at his funeral and included the story of the high school dance that night and how his one social gesture was such a milestone in my life.

I concluded Wayne's (Al's) eulogy with, "Once we were six and now we are five," referring of course to my Band of Brothers analogy. This morning, as I was finalizing these memoirs to meet with my publisher for the first time, I received a call from Ozzie that Don (Mouse) had passed away, almost two years to the day that Wayne left us. Don was a "salt of the earth" kind of guy who never spoke ill of anyone. He was a unique character and as genuine a friend as anyone could ever have. Sadly, we are now just four.

As it turned out, my initial upbeat reaction the first day of school at Okotoks was premature. Not so much from a social perspective, but my lack of scholastic confidence returned yet again. I had recovered nicely from the near failure in Grade Two to mostly As and Bs throughout elementary and junior high. But the new surroundings, starting all over again, and the increasing gap in my social skills contributed, in one way or another, to a renewed struggle.

Mom arranged for an IQ test, which seemed odd to me, especially since I hadn't asked for one. IQ tests, in my opinion, can actually do more harm than good if administered when one is simply lacking confidence. I was never given the results, but not long afterwards I was encouraged to split my Grade Twelve into two years instead of one. I did, taking the second year at Mount Royal College. I have often wondered if it was the right thing to do. Clearly, it was my decision as no one held a gun to my head. It kept me from graduating from Okotoks High and attending graduation ceremonies, and that upset me. Would I have passed if I had taken it all in one year? Would my grades have gotten worse and set me back even more? Who knows.

CHAPTER 11
Gill Stories I

Over the years, especially between ages twenty and thirty-five, I managed to be involved in situations that were funny and at times bordered on unbelievable. Most often, they were my fault because I didn't always think before I did things, or I was in the wrong place at the wrong time. In some cases, I was lucky to survive. For years, friends have suggested that I put these "Gill Stories" on paper for posterity.

Admitting failure or having done things not so well is good for the soul. In the 2004 film *Garden State,* the character Sam says, "If you can't laugh at yourself, life's gonna seem a whole lot longer than you like." This echoes my sentiments exactly. I have never lost the ability to laugh at myself. I would never have made it otherwise.

I dipped my toe into the part-time job pool during my high school and university years, what Ian Tyson, the great cowboy singer and writer, called "Summer Wages." At sixteen, Dad got me my first real paying job, painting creosote on dozens of fence posts for a neighbour. Wikipedia describes creosote as "a portion of chemical products obtained by the distillation of a tar that remains heavier than water, notably useful for its anti-septic and preservative properties." The posts were old rail ties that required treating to better withstand weather conditions. Breathing in creosote out of a pail is equivalent to siphoning gasoline out of a car with one's mouth and swallowing it. Apparently, I took longer to do the job than I was supposed to, but little wonder. After breathing the creosote fumes for half an hour while painting one post, I would then stagger to the next one, but only after taking a few minutes to locate it through the mental haze. Forget a toke of marijuana; my drug of choice was creosote fumes out of a pail. Just as effective and much longer lasting. In fact, it had a bit of a permanent feel to it.

The next part-time job was stacking bales for an old couple who had a farm about ten miles away. Dad, in his democratic style, found the job and volunteered me. It would have been nice if he had asked what I might like to do. Grocery bagging or gas jockeying had much more appeal from a less-effort-expended perspective than stacking bales. The farmer was a nice old gentleman by the name of Reg, who should have sold the farm twenty years earlier. I was hired to stack heavy hay bales on a sled while he drove the tractor.

After a couple of weeks trying to lift and stack bales that weighed more than I did, my never-to-be-developed triceps collapsed in protest and simply gave out. Unable to lift the bales anymore, I was ordered to drive the tractor while Reg stacked the bales, which was not exactly what he was paying for. The neighbours driving by no doubt wondered, "What the hell?" when they saw this kid driving the tractor and eighty-five-year-old Reg in the back trying to stack the bales. Even though there must have been at least a million bales left in the field, that night he concluded the job was finished. I was paid and relieved of my duties. (I use the words relieved and fired interchangeably.) As I drove away the next morning, I swear he had his seventy-five-year-old wife driving the tractor while he tackled the bales. A better job at no cost! I did learn one valuable lesson: delegate upward whenever possible.

Part-time job number three, again Dad's choice, was, no surprise, working for another farmer. "Does he not know anyone other than farmers?" I thought. Robert Carr was a nice guy who ran a large farm operation. The first week of work entailed driving a tractor around a field pulling a rock picker machine that would pick up rocks that had worked their way to the surface after years of plowing. When full, I would pull the picker over near the fence and dump the rocks. This job was like working at a health spa compared to the previous backbreaking job of stacking bales of hay. The next week, I got my first promotion, of sorts.

I was to cultivate the same field that I had just picked all the rocks from. Cultivating is similar to shallow plowing, preparing the soil for later seeding. This was most definitely a step up from rock picking. If there was such a thing as heaven on a farm, this was it: driving a $50,000 John Deere tractor pulling a cultivator. Starting on the outside of the field, one plows around and around in ever smaller concentric squares until the entire field is fully plowed. The hardest part is making sure the plowshares are set at the right depth to be effective but not so deep that it causes the tractor to overwork. The objective was to plant seeds, not drill for oil. Another important fact is that when a tractor pulls hard, the rear wheels do the most work. The front wheels are largely for steering and tend to ride lightly on the ground. If the rear wheels have to dig in hard to pull something, the front wheels will actually come off the ground slightly. This is normal. Around and around I went, always checking the plow behind me and occasionally looking ahead to be sure I was plowing in a straight line. The seagulls were constantly landing behind the newly plowed earth to grab any upturned worms. Life was good down on the farm. "This ain't all bad. Maybe Dad sold our farm too soon," I thought to myself.

On about the thirtieth lap around the field, I happened to look up to see a rubber inner tube lying on the ground ahead of me. "What the hell? That wasn't there the last time around." I looked down at my front wheels. To my horror, the right front tire was twisted sideways on the rim with the inner tube missing. It didn't take a degree in Agriculture to know I had spent too much time looking back instead of ahead. Somehow, the tire had twisted badly on a sharp turn. Who knew which corner and how far back. I had plowed a complete circuit of the field without noticing. "Shit!" I yelled. "This can't be good." I stopped the tractor and got off, shaking with fear for what might happen next.

"Thank God I found the tube. How would I have explained that the inner tube was missing?" I thought, not wanting to even imagine the outcome otherwise. I picked up the tube and carried it back, and then tried to get the twisted tire off the wheel. I would have had more success changing the rear tire on an eighteen-wheeler semi-truck with bare hands. There was no way to manually jam the tube back into the tire.

Robert, the nice farmer, showed up, and right before my eyes transformed into The Hulk, without the green! I avoided looking him in the eye as I tried to explain what had happened, wisely skipping the part about having made a complete revolution of the field without noticing the tire twisted on the wheel. His face was pale, his head was shaking, and I thought he was going to lose it right then and there. It was even more awkward repeating the explanation as he refused to believe it the first time, or the second, or the third. Like old Reg, Robert decided that it was best that I just move on *and* off the farm. One thing about farmers is that they are consistent. If you don't perform, you're through. There was a definite pattern developing here.

Next and last up on Dad's seemingly infinite list of part-time jobs was Golden West Farms, founded by Max Bell and Frank McMahon. Other than maybe the famous geological wonder of the Big Rock, a huge boulder outside of town that glaciers moved from the Arctic millions of years ago, the Golden West Farm was the claim to fame for the community of Okotoks. Situated just outside the town boundaries, the Golden West Farm was one of the finest Thoroughbred horse racing stables and breeding farms in all of North America, and arguably the best in Western Canada. It was of the same quality as E.P. Taylor's famous Winfield Farms outside Toronto, the home of Northern Dancer.

Max Bell was the wealthy publisher of several newspapers across Canada, including *The Calgary Albertan*. He lived in Calgary, but had a second home at the Farm. He was also very active in the community with his time and philanthropic activities, and he helped the Calgary Stampede by inviting and hosting dignitaries at the Farm, including Bing Crosby and Robert F. Kennedy.

I had a coincidental connection to Mr. Bell as a young boy on the ranch back at Throne. One Saturday, I was watching the Queen's Plate, Canada's premier horse race, on our black and white TV. I had never watched a real horse race before and was intrigued. An announcer was interviewing Mr. Bell and asked about his horse, Return Trip, who was running in the Queen's Plate. Mr. Bell explained that he had shipped a mare to France to be bred to a famous stallion and then brought the now in-foal mare back to Canada. Thus, the name of her colt was Return Trip. I never forgot his rationale for naming that colt and, to this day, I love the classic racehorse names. (Mr. Bell and the McMahon brothers, in partnership with Bing Crosby, owned a very good California horse by the name of Four And Twenty, named for the day it was born, April 20. Four And Twenty won the Santa Anita Derby in 1961.) Return Trip did not win that day—I think it was Flaming Page—but the race, the interview, and the horse stirred a new passion in me.

I couldn't believe it, but of all the horses at Golden West Farms the summer I worked there, Return Trip was one of them. Prince D 'Amour and others also stood at stud. I don't recall how many mares were stabled there, but I would guess about forty that Mr. Bell owned, plus many that were there temporarily for breeding. In addition, there were yearlings and the two year olds in training, so all in all it was a large racing operation.

This time, the job had real potential, and it actually crossed my mind that it might lead to a career as a jockey. I was eighteen and still only weighed 120 pounds. My shoe size was a problem though. As light as I was, my feet were already too large for the tiny stirrups on the riding saddle. Any aspirations for a jockey career were short lived.

Working and living at Golden West Farms was most enjoyable. True, cleaning out the stalls every day and stacking hay wasn't much fun, but it was more than offset by feeding the horses, helping with the foaling and breeding of mares, and watching the training of the two year olds. The names of the horses, like Abeyance, Acceptor, Gilmore, Vent D 'Hiver (Winter Winds), Waltzing Doll, and Merger (who would win the Queen's Plate the next year) still ring out today.

Because of my romantic fantasies about life on the track, I suggested that I might like to work at the real racetrack sometime. Immaturity really does cause dumb ideas. So, one day in early August, while loading newly trained racehorses into a horse trailer to be shipped to the track, the Farm Manager pulled me aside and said, "If you want to go to the track and work, here's your chance. You can ride with the trailer to Saskatoon."

If ever the saying "Careful what you wish for" was true, this was it. I had completely forgotten about my ill-conceived suggestion three months earlier, but there it was, staring me in the face. I was shocked and didn't want to go. I was happy on the Farm and had only a month to work before going to college. In truth, he should never have suggested it, but my guess is he had an operation to run and knowing that I was leaving in a month anyway, this was his way to reduce overhead.

From the moment I said yes, everything went downhill. There was no room in the tractor (front) of the huge truck for me to sit. I was to ride in the horse trailer with the horses, all the way to Saskatoon, some 450 miles. It's not often one gets a chance to ride in a windowless trailer, with hay bales and several standing horses for nearly eight hours. It ranked right up there with having a wisdom tooth pulled without freezing.

There wasn't enough light to read anything and there was no radio. It was just the horses, my sleeping bag, a few clothes, and I. After what seemed like a whole day, I suddenly heard a noise and the side door opened. The driver and his partner had stopped for gas and a bite to eat and generously thought that maybe the kid in the trailer, had he not suffocated, might want to eat as well. An hour later, back into the pit of hell I went, the door once again slamming shut behind me. Next stop was Saskatoon, hours away.

My mistake was reinforced immediately upon arrival in the middle of the night. After helping to unload the horses at the Golden West barn, I discovered that there wasn't a job for me. They had all the guys they needed. I had assumed there would be a job or why offer me the opportunity. I hadn't even thought to ask the question. Another lesson learned: confirm everything before saying yes. Jobs in August, after the races had already been running the circuits since May, were non-existent. Welcome to the track!

Too proud to admit my mistake and not willing to accept defeat, I decided I would try and hustle up some work each day, but first it meant finding sleeping arrangements. I ended up rolling out my sleeping bag in a vacant stall. This was not an unusual practice at the track. Common showers were provided in a separate washhouse building.

Unless you're a trainer or a groom, the scope of work available at a track is limited to one thing: hot walking. It's the lowest rung of the job ladder. Hot walking entails walking a horse around in circles for about twenty to thirty minutes until it's "cooled out" from the race. "Cooled out" is determined by a simple test. Each time you circled a tank of water, you would let the horse stop and have a short drink; when he no longer takes a drink, he is cooled out. For this, I got one dollar, or maybe two dollars if the horse had won and the trainer felt generous. Between hot walking horses early in the morning before sunrise and hot walking again late in the afternoon after the races, I might get as many as a dozen horses a day. Little wonder then that I was the most educated hot walker on the track.

Horse racing attracts its share of people who are borderline shady, but for the most part the track is full of hard-working honest people who love what they do. It did me no harm to meet and work with those who, by choice or not, were not as fortunate as I was and able to go to college. Such experience keeps one's feet on the ground for life. A real highlight was that Mr. Bell's horse, Gilmore, won the coveted Canadian Derby that year, 1967. How I wish I had been working the stable then and got to hold him in the winner's circle.

I witnessed something that summer at the races that very few can ever say they have seen, or admit to have seen. At the track that summer was a trainer by the name of Chattahoochee Smith, whom everybody loved. He was old, dirt poor, and an owner and trainer of a single horse in his stable: Sly Fox. Now, Sly Fox was no threat to any track records and, in fact, would not have won the derby at a county fair. He was in the category of the lowest claimers, about $1,500, as I recall. But old Chattahoochee loved, cared for, and trained Sly Fox like he was the next Triple Crown winner. He had to. Sly Fox's winnings were all he had to live on. Winter was coming and the race season was coming to an end, but Sly Fox's earnings had barely covered his expenses, if that. Chattahoochee was in for a long, tough winter. As I recall, Sly Fox was entered in a claiming race on the last race on the last day. No trainer dared claim the horse, for not only was he a non-winner, but it would deprive the nice old guy of his only income the next year. At post time, Sly Fox was the "longest shot" on the tote board.

"And they're off!" the track announcer blared over the loud speaker as the horses bolted from the gate. "And Sly Fox takes the early lead."

This was all new to Sly Fox! He had never been in a race when he was looking at blue sky and not the rear end of a horse. Down the backstretch they ran before rounding the far turn and heading for home.

"Sly Fox has a three-length lead," the announcer said, his voice crackling with utter surprise. "At the Finish Line it's Sly Fox winning it, pulling away!" the announcer all but screamed.

Sly Fox could have slowed to a walk and still won the race that day. Not only did Chattahoochee collect the winnings, but, rumour had it, several trainers bet on his horse and gave him their betting tickets. Old Chattahoochee now had enough to make another winter. The fix was in! I can tell this story because the Statute of Limitations has probably expired and, besides, all the key players, including the horses, have likely all died. Sometimes doing the wrong thing is the right thing to do.

"Momma didn't raise no fool," so eventually I took the hint that getting a summer or part-time job was a necessity if I hoped to have spending money or have any chance of going to college or university. Now it was up to me to find my own jobs, preferably less labour intensive and not on a tractor.

While in my first year of junior college, my classes were always in the day, so any part-time job had to be in the late afternoon or early evening. My first handpicked job was as a car jockey for the Universal Ford dealership at, as always, minimum wage. Nowadays, when you arrive to pick up your car after servicing, you go find the car on your own. "Sir, your car is ready and parked somewhere on our lot." Then, you search for your car in a sea of cars that all look the same. You check the front lot, the sides, the back. If you're really lucky, you'll find it before the warranty runs out.

Back in the '70s, car dealers had car jockeys. When the customer arrived, the car jockey grabbed the car keys from the drawer behind the counter, found the car, and drove it out to the front and held the door open. Now this was service!

"Hey, kid, go to the back and bring the yellow 1965 Meteor up to the front," the service manager barked.

"Yes, sir!" I replied, grabbing the keys and heading out.

Very quickly I found the car, a canary on wheels the size of a four-bedroom house. Not only was it huge like other models of that era, it also had the unique feature of a back window that tilted in towards the car (irrelevant to the story, but an interesting fact all the same). It had just been in for a complete repaint of bright canary yellow.

Instantly, I identified a potential problem. The car was tightly parked between two vehicles, one of them a monster truck. There was barely room to get in on either side. After incurring great pains to get into the vehicle without denting the car door, I began the process of backing out. Ever so slowly, like backing up an aircraft carrier through the Panama Canal, I backed up one foot at a time. And then there was a sound that I hadn't heard since some kid clawed his fingernails on the blackboard in Grade Three. It was a sickening sound.

I squeezed out, as painful as squeezing in, and walked around the car. The monster truck had a steel encased signal light sticking out of its left side that had caught on the side of the Meteor, inches from the back end. And I still had another twenty feet to go! I gawked at a car jockey's worst nightmare: a deep, two-inch scratch on a fresh paint job. The signal light was jammed on the side of the car so tightly that going forward or backward would just continue the scratch.

I concluded that continuing to back up was the best of the worst horrible outcomes. Logic told me I could move over far enough while backing up and limit the damage. Two inches? He'll never see it until days after he leaves, I figured. I continued to back up and *that sound* continued. But now it was go-for-broke time. There was no going backwards, figuratively speaking. Finally, the car was clear of the truck. I hopped out to assess the damage. I couldn't believe my eyes! Instead of a two-inch long scrape, there was a half-inch high scrape extending in one continuous line from the back end all the way to the front end on the passenger side. The worst juveniles in the city couldn't have keyed it better. I felt ill.

My plan was to fess up to the service manager right away, but, like the boxer who has a plan until he's knocked out by the first punch to his head, things did not unfold as expected. I drove up to the front of the dealership, passenger side opposite to the entrance. When the owner came, I abandoned my plan in favour of longevity. They say honesty is the better part of valor. I wasn't into valor, so I skipped the honesty part. I chickened out! I handed him the key and said, "Have a nice day!" and off he drove, smiling.

Guilt set in almost immediately.

A few minutes later, I had to confess. I approached the service manager. "Sir, when I backed that yellow Meteor out, I put a scratch on it. I think we better call the fellow and let him know."

"What! What happened?" he asked, still reasonably under control.

"I caught a truck signal light while backing up." It was futile to explain why or how, I decided. He was in no mood to listen to my sob story.

He called the car's owner while I stood there. "Sir, I've

been told that we put a scratch on your car while bringing it up for you. Would you mind checking it?"

The longest two minutes of my life passed until he came back on the phone to the manager.

The manager looked at me, his hand cupped over the receiver. "He says there isn't any scratch."

"Um, he should check the passenger side," I said, and then stood back, waiting for the land mine I was standing on to go off.

"I'm sorry, sir, check the passenger side. He says it's there."

Another minute passed.

I still have nightmares hearing the owner screaming in the phone. I was ten feet away, but no translation was needed. Not every word was clear, but the tone let me know he had seen the damage.

The car would need to be brought back for a new paint job, at the dealer's cost. The next day, the dealership asked me to switch to the day shift. They didn't say why, but I had a hunch they knew I was attending school during the day and it would be impossible for me to work the day shift. I got the message. Time to move on, again. Getting fired was now beginning to be a substitute for a career change.

During the summer months, I needed to work in order to

save money for the next year's university. To be successful in a career, it isn't just how bright you are; you need to get a break somewhere along the way that gives you the chance to shine or fail. The break might mean knowing the right person at the right time or hearing about a job before others. Regardless, it's still a break.

My break was having an uncle who was a field supervisor in the oilfields. Uncle Ronnie was one of my mother's six brothers, all of whom got jobs in the oil industry right out of high school. Alex, Ron, David, and Mac all worked for my parents on the ranch at one time or another to earn a bit of money before heading to the oil patch. I liked all my uncles and have fond memories of Ronnie in particular. He had taken a real liking to me, nicknaming me Louie. I have no idea why.

I asked Ron if he could get me a summer job in "the patch." He was told that the departmental budget didn't have room for summer students, but he stuck his neck out and hired me anyway as a roustabout. A roustabout job basically entailed doing the lowest manual jobs, like shovelling gravel, clearing and burning right-of-way brush, helping the welder, or whatever. No matter, it was a badly needed job for me and I jumped at it. Uncle Ron died of cancer about a dozen years later, but I will be forever grateful to him for giving me my start. His willingness to hire me started me on a forty-year career path in the oil business.

During that summer of working in the oil fields, I had my first lesson on what happens when one is just a bit too keen. I decided one evening to find an old oil well that no one seemed to ever check on. It was located in the bush about two miles off the main highway past an old farm. I was quite proud when I found the long lost well, but no sooner had I found it than my truck got stuck in the mud.

There were no cellphones in the early '70s, so I decided to walk to the farm that I had passed on the way, in the hope of making a phone call for someone to come and get me. I kept my eye out for any sign of a four-legged killer. I don't have a phobia about dogs, but I am nervous about big dogs after having been bitten by one that loved people and had never bitten anyone before. All of a sudden, around the corner of the barn, a dog came running at full speed. He had the bark and the look of a dog straight out of a K-9 unit. The only thing missing was the policeman to call him off and me not having the standard padded training gear. He was Rin Tin Tin with the demeanor of Ol' Yeller, after he got rabies!

Panic set in and I started sprinting toward the small single-story farmhouse. I had only one thought: make it to the house before the dog makes it to me! This was not a baseball game where a tie goes to the runner. A tie here was a surefire way of being tagged out for good. About ten feet from the door, with the dog gaining rapidly, I made an instant, life-saving decision. I decided to skip the courtesy knock on the door. Ol' Yeller and I hit the front porch at the same time, but I opened the door and slammed it shut behind me in time. Round One went to me!

Not fifteen feet away stood a small, silver-haired lady ironing clothes. There we were, just the two of us, like frozen mimes. I was twenty-one, totally out of breath and speechless. She was eighty, shocked and speechless. Why she didn't throw the iron at me, I don't know.

"I'm sorry, but your dog was chasing me," I squeaked out after a few seconds. Clearly, more needed to be said. "I'm stuck at a well site and wondered if I could use your phone."

"Yes," she replied timidly, no doubt thinking that I was going to use it regardless of how she answered. The tension quickly dissipated with more conversation and I made the call to the office. I was told to hitchhike back to town if I could and we'd get the truck out in the morning. "Nice, loyal co-workers," I thought.

"Thank you for letting me use your phone. I'll go out to the highway and catch a ride."

"You're welcome," she replied graciously.

Then, I remembered that the dog was outside, waiting for me to leave third base and try stealing for home. Round Two was about to begin.

"Does your dog bite?" I asked.

"Only after dark," she replied. "But I'll hold him until you get to the highway."

That was the good news. The bad news was that the sun would set in only half an hour.

Off to Surgery

Irv, Jean, Me, and Stuart

Best of Buddies

Old Fashioned
Picnic

Discussing
our Wish List

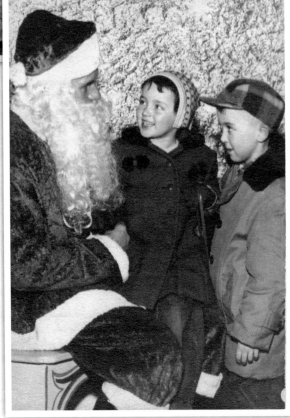

Ready for Sunday School

First Day of Grade One

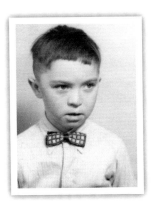

Grade Two – Not Happy!

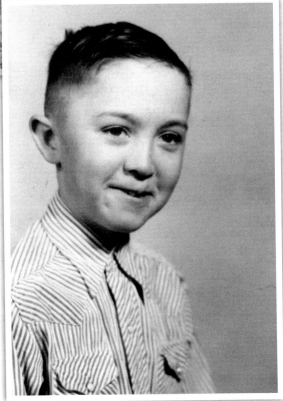

Grade Six – Happy Days

The Perfect Children

Crazy Horse, Little White Dove, and Geronimo

Christmas Morning

1958 – Irv had left for the Air Force

16 going on 13!

By The Way Ranch

Dad promoting Herefords

8 Second Ride

Traditional Branding

Grad Day – 1972

Band of Brothers
Al and Mike (top);
Me and Ozzie (Bottom)

Don, Ozzie, and me at Al's wedding

Wedded Bliss – 1984

Golfing at Carnoustie, Scotland

Biking in France

Cruising the Med!

Ready to go! – 1952

55 Years Later!

Our Proud Family

I walked the hundred yards to the highway, mostly backwards to make sure she kept her word. It's amazing how well one can walk backwards when it makes the difference between living and dying. Once I reached the top of the lane, she let go of the dog's collar and walked back into the house to finish what I had so rudely interrupted. The dog, on the other hand, sat on his haunches and observed. Somehow, I got the feeling that he had been through this before and had buried all the bodies in the backyard. He was a sadist and liked to stretch the inevitable out as long as he could. Sunset was his favourite time of day, so he was just biding his time.

Every five minutes the dog would let out a loud and deep "woof," then advance up the lane about fifty feet and sit again, all the while never taking his eyes off me. The sun was dropping like a rock and with each "woof" things got more intense. Time was on his side and he knew it. It didn't take a mathematician to figure out that eight woofs equaled me being shredded to pieces. The traffic on the highway was sparse at that time of the evening. No one stopped.

Predictably, the dog arrived just prior to sunset. I tried to balance myself with one foot on top of a two-foot high reflector post. This would be my last stand, my own Alamo. The posts were wooden and cut at a forty-five degree angle, so trying to balance on them while holding one's thumb out was nearly impossible. Cars went by and I can't imagine why they didn't stop.

Clearly the sand in the hourglass was running out to

nothing. Just then, like a miracle, I heard a large transport truck. In desperation, I jumped down, stood as far out on the highway as I dared, and waved my arms like some guy who had been lost for years and suddenly found. The sound of the air brakes was like sweet music. Once in the truck, I couldn't help but look back at the dog. His head was down as he turned and walked back to the farm. A rare defeat, no doubt.

CHAPTER 12
Confession Time

People write their memoirs for a reason. I'm fascinated by the confessions of those who supposedly free their souls of guilt, under the guise of wanting to help others avoid such pitfalls. Commendable as they may be, I've never been totally convinced of the merit of confessing in public. Then again, if it helps them deal with the issue, sell books, or keep one person from falling into the same trap, then kudos, I guess. I include the following "confession," not because it cleanses me of my sin, but because it was such a fork in the road. It was a life-changing and life-learning experience. It taught me to grant others a second chance.

It was bitterly cold the winter I attended Mount Royal College in Calgary to complete the second half of my Grade Twelve. One particularly cold day, I took the bus downtown to shop at the Hudson Bay store, then the largest department store in the city.

As I browsed around in the basement men's wear department, I came upon a bin full of earmuffs. Just what I needed. I had a pair of gloves, but nothing to wear on my head. Problem was, I didn't have a credit card or enough cash. What I did next was out of character for me, unexplainable, inexcusable, and potentially a life-changing disaster. As a teenager, you feel invulnerable, and I was no different. I was also naïve. I slipped the earmuffs into my coat pocket.

A few seconds later, a large man in a heavy coat and hat, looking like a customer but clearly not one, grabbed my elbow. "Come with me, young man," he said quietly but firmly. My heart sank and my stomach was one huge knot. As we walked, I knew I was in big trouble. My life as I knew it was over. If the bookies were taking bets, the odds would have been three to one that I'd get three to five in the slammer!

I was taken to a room in the back of the basement. It was small, cramped, and sparsely furnished. A woman was there, tall and unsmiling, sitting behind a desk. He sat beside her and ordered me to take a seat. I quickly sat in the chair, the rickety type used at card tables. No introductions were necessary or offered. The woman was obviously a store detective, as was he. I don't know how long I was there, maybe twenty minutes, but they were the longest and most excruciating minutes of my life. It was an execution by intravenous drip!

The man reached into the middle desk drawer and took out a form in triplicate: white, blue, and orange. I guessed the blue one went to the police. I was going to be charged. My mind raced, reeling from the shock and suddenness of the events. "Why did I do it? What am I going to do now? I'm in real trouble!"

As I sat in silence, I could see him filling out the incident portion of the form: time, date, location, item taken. Then the usual "Sergeant Friday" interrogation started. "Name? Age? Address? Occupation?" I answered politely, spelling my name for greater clarity.

"We saw you putting earmuffs in your pocket," he said. "Do you have anything to say?"

"Oh shit" came to mind, but wisely I replied, "Yes, sir, I did take the earmuffs and I apologize. It's cold outside and I just took them. I'm very sorry. It was a dumb mistake."

Then, the woman spoke, or barked, really. "Well, you should have thought about that before you took them. It's too late now." I guess she had already rendered me a petty criminal.

"Hey, easy there! He's being honest. He's admitted to taking them," the man snapped. For some reason, I detected a soft spot in his heart.

After some silence, more dialogue, more silence, he leaned over the desk and said, "Son, because you were honest and confessed to taking the earmuffs, I'm not going to lay charges. We'll keep this form on file in case you ever do such a thing again. Do you understand what I'm telling you?"

"Yes, I do, and thank you. I've made a terrible mistake and I've learned from it."

. He stood up and said I could go on my way. I trembled as I walked out of the office, through the basement, up the escalator, and out the store to the nearest bus stop.

I have never forgotten that black day in my life. Needless to say, I have never since taken even as much as a bar of soap from a hotel bathroom (although my wife does!). I have never satisfactorily answered the question of why I had such a sudden lack of judgement. I was raised to be honest and, to this day, I wonder what would have happened had the detective charged me. I'm sure it would have negatively affected my future and career success. Mistakes like this have a habit of sticking with you. If the detective is still alive, I thank him for taking the high road and giving a teenager a second chance. I will be forever indebted.

CHAPTER 13
The Great Pretender

During the late '60s and early '70s, my social life continued to be as active as a sloth race. I had made lifelong friends, but dating was still non-existent. I was still skinny and still had the severe speech impediment and facial features that left a lot to be desired. When it came to dating girls, I was simply too shy and lacked the confidence to ask anyone out. Hanging out with the guys was the best. Whether going to a movie, snowmobiling, golfing, or just having a few beers, these were my happiest moments.

But this was also when the guys were sowing their wild oats, totally normal for young men in their late teens and early twenties. To their immense credit, they always included me whenever they could. I was grateful for that. Without this inclusion, I might have withdrawn completely. I hate to think of where I would be (or not be) if they hadn't kept me socially involved.

One of the biggest social occasions is New Year's Eve. While Christmas is traditionally a family affair, New Year's Eve is an adult celebration, a time to party with friends and a special date. But New Year's Eve always presented a real challenge for me during those drought years of dating. The closer it came, the more anxious I became.

One New Year's Eve took me down to one of my lowest depths of depression. Not a suicidal depression, but a sadness that ate away at me. Loneliness is a horrible thing when it isn't your choice. As the day approached, it was clear there was no party for me to attend, no date to accompany me. All of my friends were going on dates or double dates.

I had pride and was determined that no one would feel sorry for me. The last thing I wanted was for anyone, most of all my parents, to think that I had nothing to do on New Year's Eve. That would be admitting failure. Pride trumped everything. Still, I couldn't bring myself to stay at home. I made up a story about having a date and a party to go to and asked my parents if I could borrow the family car. I didn't own a car like most of my friends did, so my transportation choices were limited. If I were truly going on a date, hitchhiking would have been a giveaway that the whole evening was a sham. However, asking to borrow the car ranked right up there with being water-boarded!

It was around seven o'clock and Dad was lying on the chesterfield in the kitchen, his favourite nap place, when I mustered up enough courage to pose the question. I sat behind him, not wanting to look him in the eyes.

"Can I have the car tonight?" I asked.

"Why do you need the car?" His tone already told me his preferred answer.

"I'm going to meet someone and attend a party."

A long pause. "Jeepers, I don't know," he said, followed by another long pause. "You know, I always knew that Stuart and Jean would want the car, but I never thought you would."

I was stunned. I was already struggling with not actually having a date (that night or any night) or a party to go to, but to be told by my father that he didn't expect me to date hurt my feelings. "I'm no different than Stuart or Jean," I thought to myself. "I want to go out too."

Dad would never intentionally hurt my feelings, but in his mind what he said was a true assessment of the situation. In many ways, he was supportive, but he rarely grasped my need for encouragement. I knew he was speaking the truth, but why say it so bluntly? I wanted so badly to be normal that I refused to accept that I wasn't, except for moments like this. It still stings to this day, over forty years later.

"Okay, go ahead if you must," he said reluctantly.

As I pulled out of the garage, I thought, "Now what?" I had nowhere to go. Whatever I chose to do, it had to take me past midnight. I also couldn't be seen by anybody who knew me. So *what does* a socially challenged single guy with a big car and no date do on New Year's Eve?

I headed to the city. It didn't take long to decide to go to a drive-in theatre. It would eat up time and I wouldn't be seen. Sandy Posey's 1950s song "Sad Movies" applied to me big time. I don't recall the movie that night, but I do recall the loneliness of sitting in the car with only my buttered popcorn and Coke. Millions of people may have traded places with me, including the homeless, the terminally ill, and the hungry, but to a teenager, this was as bad as it could get. Just before midnight, before the movie's end, I backed up the car and headed for the exit.

On the way home, I stopped at Bar X for something to eat and to waste more time. The Bar X was a chain of steak restaurants where the food was served cafeteria-style to keep the costs down. Normally, I would wolf down the food, but somehow I managed to stretch out the meal to well past one o'clock.

So many things from that night played havoc with my psyche, from being challenged on borrowing the car to silently waiting for time to pass. The evening wasn't the end of the world, but it certainly was a low point in my life.

CHAPTER 14
Change in Course

Most of us can look back on our lives and pick a year that ranked at the lowest end of the scale for positive outcomes. If Grade Two was my lowest as a child, then 1968 was a close second. It was my "Annus Horribilis."

The stage had been set four months earlier when I entered Engineering School at university. Like all the other new Engineering students, I was seated in a large theatre-style auditorium, anxiously looking forward to the Dean's welcoming message and a few words of encouragement. We were all embarking on the most important journey of our lives, to that point, and his words would be important.

Not two minutes into the speech, he said, "Everyone, look at the person on your right and then on your left." Then, after a short pause, he said, "Remember who they are because two out of three of you will not be here next spring." Clearly, the Dean had never heard of Tony Robbins' motivational techniques. I had yet to attend one class or even open a textbook, but somehow I knew that I would be one of the failures. It was only a matter of time.

Sure enough, when January 1968 arrived, the "Please See the Dean" list was posted in the hallway. To us, the list of the *inevitable to fail* was a brand for life. It didn't just list our ID numbers, so one could slip away silently and anonymously (until the anointed ones figured out who was missing in class), but our actual names. As I anxiously looked down the list of names in alphabetical order, I prayed there would be no "Gs". But my eyes soon fell on "Gillard, Douglas." I had made the list no one wanted to make.

I knew what *seeing* the Dean meant. We all did. Who was he kidding? Unlike Custer, we knew a massacre coming when we saw one. The chat was his way of suggesting, rather firmly, that we may want to consider a different career choice and not waste four more months confirming what he already knew. "You can stay if you like, but frankly . . ." Following this uplifting message was an already booked appointment with the university student counsellor. They anticipated everything!

The counsellor, nice, soft-spoken, with perfect instinct, asked, "How do you think your family will take the news?"

I had toughened up a lot over the years and had managed to control my emotions, but for the first time since almost failing Grade Two, I had failed. I broke down and cried. There was no sugar-coating the result. It was what it was and I was embarrassed. I had been in control of my outward feelings for too long, all the while having serious inward feelings, but now the jig was up. I replied to the effect that I was worried about disappointing them and letting them down. And, frankly, I was scared.

I still recall Dad's reaction that day when I got home and

told him I'd be dropping out of Engineering. Almost certainly the counsellor had called them ahead and had a chat about how to be supportive. There was no rallying cry for another "Charge of the Light Brigade," but there was also no surprise or disappointment either. He said, "Well, these things happen." For once, it was the right thing to say.

I had no business choosing engineering as a career. I had no idea what it entailed and I didn't even like engineering. Although bright enough to handle the challenge, there was no escaping the fact that I was just too socially and scholastically immature to handle such a difficult curriculum. Certainly, engineering is a challenge for anyone, at any age or background, but my chances of success would have been much greater had I waited a couple of years. Even the extra year of high school hadn't added the sufficient maturity to handle the dedication required.

In the middle of final exams in Grade Nine, Dad took an unusual interest in how my studying was going. We were driving somewhere and he thought I should have stayed back and studied instead of going with him. He asked, "What will you do if you don't pass?" It was his way of reminding me that education was important and that I should make sure I passed my tests. I did.

Well, that moment had now arrived for real. What would I do now? I needed a change of scene. I needed to *find myself.*

I was in a rudderless dinghy adrift on a sea of uncertainty, insecurity, and immaturity. It was time to step up to the plate and take my rightful place. But the real problem was "What Place?"

So in 1968, at age twenty, I took the train to Comox with Irv, who happened to be passing through Calgary on his way back home. I had no clue what I was going to do when I got there, except that Irv and his wife, Elaine, had offered to let me stay with them a few days and look around for a job. Irv was in the Air Force (RCAF) and worked at the base just a couple of miles from their trailer.

The only way for me to get around was to hitchhike since Irv needed to drive their only car to work. On the second day of hitchhiking back from town to the trailer, a very nice corporal picked me up on his way to the RCAF Base. I mentioned that my brother was in the Air Force and that I was looking for a job. As luck would have it, the corporal worked in the Officers' Mess (the dining room and snack bar for commissioned officers, mostly pilots for fighter jets, submarine hunters, and search and rescue planes). He told me there was a job available as a dishwasher. "It isn't much," he said, "but it's a start. If you're interested, you can apply."

To his surprise, I showed up at the mess the next day. In my mind, there was no downside. I needed to make some money, so why not do this until something better showed up? Surely something would. It was just a matter of time, or so I thought.

The job qualifications were minimal. You needed to stand up, have two hands, and know the difference between a crystal glass and a metal pot. Having met those standards with flying colours, I was offered the job at $1.25 per hour plus a shared room in the barracks on the base and a meal while on shift. It wasn't much, but it was a start. I accepted.

The job actually entailed much more than just washing dishes. Somewhere buried in the KP Duty job description, written in small print, were other duties, including peeling potatoes and washing the floor and equipment. Not surprisingly, I mastered the art of dishwashing, re-stacking dishes, and washing floors in one day. I might have flunked Engineering, but this I could handle!

Peeling potatoes was the easiest and nothing like when I peeled them on the farm for supper. I poured about thirty potatoes in what looked like an upright clothes spinner, shut the lid, and turned it on. The face of the inside of the spinner was a gravel-type substance which, when water was sprayed in continuously, knocked the skin off the potatoes as they were spun around inside. After a couple of minutes, you stopped the spinning, emptied the potatoes, and started over again.

Boredom set in within hours. Soon, I was befriending the cooks to see what I could learn. Over the next few weeks, they took me under their wing whenever I had a few minutes to spare. Somehow, they seemed to know that dishwashing might not be that challenging for someone of university potential. I didn't get to help out on the main dining room food prep very much, but they welcomed me with open arms in the short order kitchen. The short order kitchen served up the usual fare of burgers, fries, salads, soups, and sandwiches. More and more, the chefs taught me the art of short-order cooking. I love the pressure and thrill of fast-paced food prep and cooking. I figured if I ever became unemployed, I could always flip burgers to pay the bills.

Bobby Kennedy was running for the leadership of the Democratic Party in 1968. I had developed an interest in politics and history, especially American, and was particularly interested in Bobby Kennedy. Not only because he had once stayed at the Golden West Farm, but also because he wanted to continue his brother John's vision. I was pulling for him to win the Democratic nomination for the Presidency and had purchased the paperback version of his book *Promises to Keep,* published the year before. I was in the midst of reading it when he was assassinated on June 5. I put the book away, half read, never to open it again. The passion was gone. Now, some forty years later, I still have some unfinished business to take care of.

One event that stands out that year was really a non-event, but still had a lasting influence on me. I had only been working for a few weeks when Jean announced she was getting married. I really wanted to attend, but I was saving what little money I had to return to university. I couldn't afford to fly home and I had no vacation days.

I decided to at least have a conversation with Sergeant Jarvis, head of the Officers' Mess, about going home for the wedding. I figured I needed a week. If he granted permission, then just maybe I could get Mom and Dad to help with the costs. He reacted as if I had just asked to be promoted to Head Chef.

"You want to what? You've only been here a few weeks!"

I sat in silence. Finally, he said, "OK, how much time do you need? You know it will be unpaid leave?"

Unpaid leave or not, my heart kept saying that I should go. I wrote a letter to Mom and Dad, explaining my situation. I still have the letter and have read it many times, each time seeing the change that was occurring in me. For the first time, I was becoming resentful about just how much I had to do on my own. There was even a bit of feeling sorry for myself, which was rare for me and never a good thing. Although my letter lacked maturity, it was firm in explaining my reason for not attending. I could read between the lines and see a cry for help, both morally and financially.

I never made it to Jean's wedding, but I know Mom and Dad weren't mean spirited. It just never crossed their minds to help me out by sending some money. Jockeys get on a racehorse by getting a leg up to the saddle by the horse's trainer. I never felt that I got that leg up. Always having to find my own box to stand on made me fiercely independent and, in the bigger scheme of things, it was a good thing.

CHAPTER 15
Back on Track

Washing dishes at minimum wage does something to one's psyche. There was plenty of time to think—beyond how clean the dishes were or where the floor mop was kept.

By mid-summer, I had decided to return to university and pursue a Commerce (Business) Degree. Arts was out (I had no creative thinking). Education was out (speaking clearly was a job requirement). Medicine was a non-starter given my failed foray into Engineering. Commerce seemed to best match my interests and natural aptitude. In May, I wrote a personal letter to Dr. Robinson, Dean of Business, requesting that I be allowed to apply to attend that fall.

I was accepted. Finally, a highlight amidst too many negative events.

It was like I had a new lease on life. I had saved about $600 from my dishwashing job and then applied to the government for a student loan. Tuition was $444 (cheap by today's standards) and by staying at my grandma's place, I was nearly able to support myself. Out of necessity, I asked Mom and Dad for a bit of financial help to get me to the $1,500 I figured I would need for the full university year. They came through. As was expected of me, I repaid all of their university assistance in full after graduating.

The first year of Commerce was comprised of Arts courses; the second year was a combination of Arts and Commerce. The third and fourth years were strictly Commerce, usually with a stronger emphasis on courses matching a chosen major and minor.

Theoretically, when one decides which major to choose from among finance, accounting, marketing, and business systems, one considers all factors, including what offers the best chance of a permanent job upon graduation. Like a lot of students, I didn't have a clue what the real business world looked like or how it functioned. What does an accountant really do? What do people in finance really do?

Given my speech impediment, accounting was a natural, at least in everyone else's eyes. Number crunching (or bean counting) as a backroom accounting clerk would offer me a better chance to succeed than a marketing career that required good communication skills. But, when I spoke (in my mind) I enunciated my words perfectly. I had always behaved normally since I was a kid and had never shied away from things just because of a communication issue. Speech impediment or not, I liked people and was increasingly outgoing, so why not choose marketing? I chose marketing!

This time around, things were different. I had started to mature and catch up to others my age. I was taking courses that I truly enjoyed. By year three, I had made new friends. My comeback was in full swing. Each year my confidence grew, which my grades reflected, culminating in a 3.5 average out of 4.0 in my final year. Not Rhodes scholarship material, but respectable all the same.

Midway through our fourth and final year of university, everyone began to focus on obtaining a full-time job upon graduation. My first foray into applying for a marketing position had resulted in the unsettling Texaco interview that had tested my resilience and staying power.

Consistent with the pattern I had developed over the years, my first reaction was to keep it to myself and keep smiling despite everything going to hell. The day after the Texaco interview, John Robinson, a new friend and fellow classmate, asked me how the interview went. Everyone took an interest in everyone else back then; we all hoped our classmates would get a job and go on and do well. This time, I answered from my heart, and explained, rather sheepishly, how I didn't get the job and didn't even have a real interview.

John reacted with disbelief. Word soon spread among all my classmates and, within a day, John informed me that they were drawing up a petition. Nearly all the upcoming business graduates signed a letter to Texaco protesting my treatment and categorically stating that they would refuse to interview or accept employment with Texaco. Their show of solidarity, friendship, and loyalty, at the risk of their own careers, remains with me as if it happened only yesterday. Their act of defiance spoke volumes about the importance they placed on fairness. A few weeks later, I received a letter of apology from Texaco, signed by the Senior Vice President of Human Resources. No re-interview opportunity and no job offer, just an apology. I regret not keeping and framing the letter. If ever I needed a reminder to stay focused on the positive, that was it.

It was the 1970s, long before much of the discrimination legislation that exists today. Today, this type of outright discrimination is illegal, but even if the laws had existed back then, I doubt I would have pursued the case. Regardless of what one can achieve through the courts, discrimination only disappears when people truly believe that it's wrong. Legislation helps with obvious discrimination, but does nothing for subtle discrimination. Discriminators can simply mask their actions by choosing more legitimate reasons, such as "Sorry, but we're looking for someone who has between three and three and a half years of experience."

After years of executive experience, I now give credit to Texaco for their honesty and forthrightness. The marketing job required good communication skills that, frankly, I didn't have at the time. They could have just sent me the standard Dear John letter saying that I didn't get the job and good luck in my career. Brutal as it was, knowing why I never got the job was probably better than being told a lie. Understanding reality is important to succeed, although I still believe the company made a mistake in not giving me an opportunity. Years later, I would have an opportunity to prove my point.

CHAPTER 16
Gill Stories II

My year at Mount Royal College was not just about bad judgement and petty theft. One of the most memorable and funny moments came while commuting to college from Okotoks, where I still lived with my parents.

Don "Hap" Milligan, Alan "Tank" Norris, and I were attending Mount Royal at the same time and, since we were all from Okotoks, it made sense that we carpool to and from college. I'd drive one week (in Dad's Oldsmobile), Tank one week (in his dad's car), and then Hap (in his own red, two-door Oldsmobile Cutlass). The cycle would repeat itself until the school year was concluded.

On this particular day, it was Hap's turn to drive. We decided to stop and pick up a few pizzas at Tom's House of Pizza. We were soon out on the main highway and out of the city when we realized that we hadn't picked up any Coke. There was an Esso service station south of the city, situated just off the highway on top of a little knoll, maybe a hundred yards up a gentle slope. Hap pulled up and we all bailed out of the car. I was sitting in the back and had to climb over the folded down driver's seat, typical of a two-door.

In no time, we were all walking back out the service

station door, Cokes in hand, ready to continue the trip and finish our pizzas.

"Okay, you guys. Who moved the car?" Hap asked. To do so would have been pure magic given we were never out of his sight.

"I didn't touch it," Tank and I replied in unison.

"Well, where the hell is it? It has to be here!" His tone was high and tense. I don't think he believed us. Like Indian scouts looking for the troops, the three of us spread out to look for the missing Cutlass. It couldn't have been stolen in that short a time, we each silently concluded.

After about a minute of searching, I looked over and saw Hap pick up something rather large near the light post. He held it up and calmly said, "Here's the door." This was surreal. We had a car *door* but no *car*. I couldn't believe what I was seeing.

"Where the hell is the car?" we all asked. Then, we saw something shiny across the highway in the ditch. It was the Cutlass, all right, missing door and all. It had rolled backwards on its own, void of driver or passengers, down the slope of the exit road, across the busy highway, and into the ditch on the other side; but not before clipping the light post and snapping off the passenger side door that had been left open. How it crossed the highway without a major accident is beyond my thinking capabilities. It could have been disastrous; instead, it was actually funny.

Immediately, the blame game of "Who dunnit?"

commenced. Hap and Tank asserted that I must have gotten out "that side" and left the door open. Putting my layman lawyer hat on, I declared there were two fundamental flaws with their hypothesis. First, how about some blame on the driver who had left the car in neutral in the first place, on a hill, causing it to roll backwards? Correct me if I'm wrong, but no doubt *that* was a contributing factor! Second, I got out the driver's side door not the passenger side. "So, Tank, it's your fault, not mine," I countered.

Clearly, the argument was inconclusive. After a few laughs, we jammed the door in the backseat, piled back into the car, and continued our journey home. Even John Steinbeck could not have adequately described the scene of us driving down the highway. Hap at the wheel, Tank in the passenger seat with no door, just a wide-open space, both casually eating pizza and drinking Coke. The Distracted Driver Law had not yet been enacted! It was certainly a first for me, sitting in the backseat with a car door laying beside me and a sixty-mile-an-hour wind roaring in. Try eating pizza and drinking Coke in a wind tunnel. My cheeks were ballooned out like a chipmunk wearing an oxygen mask.

Forty years later, some doubt has crept into my mind about which side I actually got out on. The best I can hope for now is a hung jury.

The early '70s weren't all work and no play.

Snowmobiling had started to boom as a recreation sport on the prairies. No longer just a workhorse for the loggers and the few farmers that could afford them, snowmobiles were being designed for speed and sport.

Unlike my buddies Ozzie and Al, I didn't own my own snowmobile. But, I did have access to one that a good friend of Dad's stored at our place. It was a "workhorse" model, probably built by a tractor manufacturer and even had a reverse gear. Ozzie and Al had "sport" models that were lightweight, sleek, and fast.

One day, Al asked Oz and me to bring our machines out to his dad's farm to have some fun. "My brother has a new half-ton truck with a loading ramp, so I'll come to your house, Gill, and we'll load it up and bring it over to my place." In no time, Al was at our farm with his brother's new truck. We set up the wooden ramp and Al drove the big machine up the ramp and into the back. The ramp was thrown in on the side and we were off.

The late afternoon and early evening went by quickly as we roared the snowmobiles around Al's parents' farm. It was amazing I wasn't decapitated when I rounded the farmhouse at full and reckless speed, only to see a wire clothesline hanging at throat level. I caught sight of it just as I raised my head up to see better. I ducked instantly! The wire neatly caught the top of my wool toque and clipped it off, which proves that it is possible for one to be fearless, stupid, and lucky all at the same time.

After several hours of fun, darkness set in and it was time to reload my snowmobile and take it home. The ramp was properly placed at about a forty-five-degree angle, with Oz and Al standing on each side to help me guide the snowmobile up and into the back of the truck. I had to have the perfect speed to climb the ramp and stop instantly once on the truck deck. My first attempt was too timid. I wasn't moving fast enough, so I stalled out halfway.

"Gill, you've got to take a better run at it than that," Oz said.

"OK! OK!" I replied and drove away.

Oz and Al continued to stand beside the ramp, shooting the breeze, awaiting my return.

There is no dispute that I needed more speed to climb the ramp. What is in dispute is how far back I drove to build up enough speed to make it on the second attempt. Ozzie claims he saw me turning the snowmobile around about a quarter mile away. He and Al were stunned to see me coming at them so fast.

By the time I hit the ramp, I was doing close to Mach One. I will never forget the look on Al and Ozzie's faces as I zipped by. Reaching the ramp at this speed had two results. One, I made it up the ten-foot ramp with no problem. Two, I overcame gravity. Houston, we have liftoff! It is an absolute fact that I never touched the bottom deck of the truck. I was Evel Knievel in a Warren Miller ski film. I hit the top part of the cab at full speed, reaffirming yet another fact: brakes need to be on the ground to be effective. Not only did I hit the cab hard, but I was at such a height that my front skis hit first and then slipped down between the cab and the box. The new half-ton was dented everywhere. I looked down at Al & Ozzie from high above the truck floor. The three of us stared at each other, speechless.

I wondered how I would explain this to Al's brother, Brian. Not surprisingly, my mind was a complete blank, much like it must have been when I had hit the ramp at warp speed. In hindsight, I think if I had gone just a bit faster I would have cleared the cab altogether and landed on the ground in front. There is always such a fine line between success and failure! Brian soon came out of the house. He had witnessed the whole thing. After recovering from the shock, he helped us lift the snowmobile *straight up* to free the front skis jammed behind the truck cab and set it back down on the truck floor. Afterwards, all we could do was laugh. I stopped laughing when the reality of paying for the truck damage set in.

I don't think there's ever been a car quite like the 1960s Chevrolet El Camino, before or since. Butch had one. It was a unique hybrid. Not half electric and half gas, but half car and half truck. Built on a Chevrolet car chassis, the front end looked and drove exactly like a car while the back end resembled the box of a half-ton truck. The truck half was limited to light loads, but nevertheless it was practical in its own way, especially for hauling stuff.

The annual tube float down the nearby Sheep River was the best informal and impromptu event of the summer in the early '70s. It was usually held on a Sunday in late June or early July when the river was still flowing fairly fast, clear, and high, but had calmed down from the muddy spring runoff. The gang would meet up with their inner tubes that they'd rounded up on their farms, borrowed from others, or bought as patched up old ones from the nearest garage. We'd all arrive at a designated spot on a bluff overlooking the river. From there, we'd roll our inflated tubes down the steep but manageable slope to the river. We'd make a second trip back up and down again with beer and wine to sustain us during the four-hour float. It really wasn't about getting a tan, floating down a river. It was all about having a good time. A drowning was considered a party spoiler.

"Gill," Butch said on the phone. "Why don't you come by my house and help me take my tube to the river."

"No problem." There was nothing I liked better than being with my buddies.

What I saw when I arrived was unexpected. Instead of a round inner tube like mine and everyone else's, Butch had an inflatable raft that could have easily met the standards for Grand Canyon raft tours. Butch was going tubing in style with zero chance of running out of beer and wine while he floated. He had already blown it up, so it was just a matter of getting it to the river.

Throwing *my* inner tube in the back of the El Camino was easy, but how to load such a huge raft required some serious planning. It was too long to fit in the back. Butch had a brilliant solution. "We'll lean the pointed front end up on the roof of the car, pointing forward, and leave the rear part of it at the back of the truck box. We'll loosely tie the back end down. Gill, you can stand on the back of it and hold down the front end while I drive." Like a good soldier, I dutifully followed orders and hopped into the back to hold the raft down.

Butch slowly backed out of the tree-lined driveway. Then, in slow gear, he headed down the residential street to the main street that would lead us to the turnoff to the river, some two miles away. What a sight it must have been. An El Camino with a river raft, fully inflated, flat side down, sticking over the top of the cab at a forty-five-degree angle, with some guy standing in the back leaning forward with two arms stiffly braced to keep the raft from falling off. Butch had his side window rolled down as a crude communication medium between the two of us.

The first 500 feet went swimmingly. I could feel a little breeze at my face as we headed towards the rendezvous point.

"Everything's okay," I yelled.

Butch went on to become a lawyer as opposed to an aeronautical engineer. I make this point since neither he, nor I for that matter, were clearly familiar with the aerodynamics of a rubber raft on top of a moving vehicle. With everything going according to plan while driving slowly, Butch determined that a little more speed was justified.

At ten miles an hour I could feel "lift" on the front end that must have been similar to what Orville Wright felt at Kitty Hawk. The raft all of a sudden had a mind of its own and wanted to rise up into the breeze. Exerting more of my weight forward, I managed to steady it down, but was feeling more anxious by the second.

Butch, of course, looking only through the rear window and seeing the raft still there, concluded there was no reason not to get to the best river spot ahead of all others. At five miles per hour, we had a steady state. At ten miles per hour, there were indications of trouble. At thirty, I went from common labourer to NASA astronaut, screaming, "We have liftoff!"

The Russian dog Laika and I had something in common. At thirty pounds, she had as much chance of keeping Sputnik II from lifting off as I, at 140 pounds, did at keeping Butch's raft from becoming airborne. It instantly transformed from a heavy, cumbersome boat to a paper airplane, carrying me straight out the back. Houston we have a problem! Grabbing at anything I could, I managed to catch a small cord inside the raft. They say you see the white light of heaven when you're about to die. As always, I was the exception. What I saw was pure hell as the raft and I slammed onto the pavement. In an instant, the raft reached the end of its tether, that long piece of rope we had so wisely decided to loosely tie to the truck box. Now I was being dragged at thirty miles an hour down the street, half in and half out of the raft. Butch finally looked out the back window and stopped. I was shaken, bruised, and scraped, but alive to fly another day. The first miracle of the day had just happened.

Everyone was already at the river meeting point. I started rolling my five-foot-high tube down the steep slope to the river. I attribute what happened next to the lingering effects of my brush with death just minutes earlier. As the tube rolled down the slope, I walked down along its side, keeping it under control. I guess the tube was heavier than I had calculated, as once again gravity took over. As the tube accelerated, I had to take longer and longer downward steps to maintain pace. Soon, the steps turned into strides, then into hops, and then into jumps. I fell, skidded, and flipped over twice during the last thirty feet down. The tube proceeded on its own volition, turning and twisting and bouncing to the river, remarkably not killing anyone. What I had not scraped, cut, or bruised an hour earlier on Main Street was now taken care of. The fact that I didn't hit my head on a rock and or drown after hitting the river headfirst was the second miracle of the day.

Finally, I was on my tube and floating. My two near-death experiences were worth it. Bruce Bolton had ingeniously roped six tire tubes and a sheet of plywood together. Throw on a cooler full of beer and we had a floating bar that rivaled any pub in town! At times of need we'd paddle ourselves near *the bar* to put in our order. The river flowed gently and the beer flowed easily as we all floated down the Sheep on that warm summer day. I don't know if it was the heat of the day or celebrating surviving two accidents, but I over imbibed. At my weight, two beers were fine; three beers were pushing it. Any more turned me into a floating zombie. I fell off the tube holding my fifth beer. I didn't want to spill any precious beer, so I held onto the bottle as I submerged under the fast flowing water. My bottle hit a rock and shattered. Once back onboard the tube, it wasn't long before I detected blood. The broken glass had sliced my finger, almost in two. Mercifully, I concluded that it would be best if this day came to an end. Given little choice, I kept the finger in the water to keep it clean until we reached the final destination where I had left my car earlier that morning. A call to the local GP at his home convinced him to meet me at his office, which was closed on Sundays, for some stitches.

The day was *finally* over. I had been thrown out of a moving car, fallen down thirty feet of rock slope, and nearly sliced my finger off, all in one day.

Apparently, one needs to *perform* three miracles to be considered for canonization. Technically, mine were *survival* miracles, but nevertheless my application to sainthood is pending. I haven't had a reply, but I'm sure it's still in the Pope's In Basket.

Towing a car is tricky. One might think it's simple

enough, but it takes nerve, concentration, and experience; none of which I possessed at the time.

Most Sunday nights were movie nights for Ozzie, Butch, Al, and me. Al and Ozzie were working, but Butch and I were still going to university. Often, the entire week would go by without seeing each other, so Sunday night, after family dinners, was our boys' night out. Each time, around five or six o'clock, someone would initiate the phone calls to get the ball rolling. The routine was the same: pick the movie, pick the time, pick who was driving.

That week, Butch initiated the process but, typical of Butch, there was always a hitch. Nothing was routine when it came to Butch. Someone always needed a ride or he needed to run an errand, take your pick. One summer Sunday night, he threw us a new one.

"Would you mind driving tonight?" Butch asked. By then I had a 1962 Pontiac Laurentian that Dad had bought me the year before for $600. "Another thing," Butch said. "Would you mind towing my car into the city on the way so I can leave it at a garage?" He got me again!

It was agreed we'd all meet at Butch's parents' house in Okotoks, twenty-five miles south of Calgary. Butch had the tow rope ready, thick and forty feet in length, but no rubber tire in the middle for tension flexibility. The movie was at seven-thirty, so there was no time to waste getting things perfect. Of all the cars I might have had to tow, Butch's car couldn't have been a worse choice. It was a British 1958 Prefect, green, and heavy as an armored tank.

We decided that Al would ride with Butch in the towed Prefect and Ozzie would ride with me. Off we went, very slowly at first to tighten the rope. We were joined at the bumpers and the wheel axels. My Pontiac was a big car, but it was no tow truck, so shifting gears and getting up some momentum took time and distance. It also took some getting used to. Ozzie, of course, provided unsolicited advice.

"Slow down. Speed up. Brake now," he'd say non-stop. As we headed north on the two-lane highway, things were looking good until we came up behind a farmer driving slower than we were. We had a movie to catch, so I made an executive decision to pull out and pass the truck. The look on Ozzie's face was indescribable, but nothing compared to the look on Butch and Al's faces in my rearview mirror. They may have been forty feet back, but I could clearly see the colour drain from their faces. I could even read their lips screaming, "You can't pass!"

The Towing Safety Manual undoubtedly states that the first rule of towing is "No passing under any circumstances." Rule number two must be "If you do pass, you better be darn sure you're successful." True to form, I underestimated the time it took to get the two-car tandem up to passing speed. Even more problematic, I underestimated how fast the farmer was driving and now there was an oncoming vehicle approaching us. It was time for corrective action. Having made it by the farmer in the old truck, who seemed to have found a fifth gear all of a sudden, I headed back into the right lane. This was well and good, except Butch and Al were still out in the left lane beside the truck, fighting desperately to keep the car from sideswiping the farmer's truck, all the while staring at an oncoming car. The farmer must have been stunned at what he saw out his left window. But for the grace of God, and the farmer, things would have ended badly. The farmer hit his brakes, allowing the towed car to pull in behind me. If you're still alive, Mr. Farmer, please accept our belated thanks. It was a completed pass!

Everything returned to normal as we continued on our merry way to the city, but for one more and even trickier maneuver. The two-lane highway met up to the main four-lane highway at a right angle, stop sign and all. We needed to cross the four-lane highway, something else that wasn't in the manual. Making matters worse was the southbound traffic coming over a rise at high speeds. The slight hill made seeing the cars a real challenge to get across in time *and* I was towing someone.

Unlike the voluntary passing of the farmer, there was no choice here. We were the African wildebeests jammed at the riverbank, knowing we must cross, even though we faced sure death.

Ozzie yelled, "Hit it!"

We knew better than to look back and see Butch and Al's faces. By now they knew they were along for the ride, like it or not. There were no cellphones to call us and protest. It quickly became evident that the lack of a rubber tire on the rope between the two cars meant zero tension flexibility. The rope had slackened when we came to a full stop, to the point where most of it rested on the pavement between us. A tire would have lessened the risk of the rope snapping, much less the necks of those in the towed car. All we could hope for was that the rope would hold. I threw the car in first gear, hit the gas hard, and fired out across the four-lane from a dead stop. The rope snapped straight, instantly jerking the front end of Butch's car off the ground, but it held! Ozzie had made a good call. We all made it across just as a southbound car roared past behind us.

Nowadays, even pulling a Red Flyer wagon gives me an anxiety attack.

CHAPTER 17

Jokes

There are all kinds of jokes out there—billions probably—about religion, race, creed, nationality, gender, profession, and on it goes. Unfortunately, many are not appropriate.

After legally coming of drinking age, then twenty-one, we would visit the Willington Hotel bar on a Saturday night once or twice a month. The place was jammed to the rafters and a country band was always playing. The lead singer of the band, Larry, whom I happened to get to know at Mount Royal a few years earlier, was from another small western town. Hearing him and his band play was sort of neat.

We were at a table in the back and everyone was talking loudly to overcome the noise. Then, during a pause between songs, I heard Larry say, "Did you hear the one about the guy with the harelip? Well, there was this guy with a harelip, you see . . ." and he went on with the joke, attempting his best to nasally enunciate like a guy with a harelip. I was stunned. I had never heard a joke about harelips and didn't even know they existed. His attempt at *talking funny* embarrassed me.

"Do I sound that bad?" I wondered. "Do people think I'm stupid?" Everyone at my table who heard it was noticeably uncomfortable and ignored the joke. It's hard to fathom, but I honestly don't believe that Larry made the connection between the joke and me. I couldn't help but wonder if harelip jokes were common? Like, where have I been?

I never heard another harelip joke until many years later at a banquet of some three dozen golfers after a friendly Ryder Cup match. After dinner, the master of ceremonies encouraged people to "get up and tell a joke." Sitting beside me was an older gentleman, who was well into his fifth martini. He stood up and everyone stopped talking to listen.

"Well, there was Ollie, the stupid Norwegian with the harelip, you see, and . . ."

It got worse. I couldn't believe what I was hearing. I couldn't tell who he was insulting more, the Norwegians or clefted people. And again, the connection between stupid and the harelip! I looked down at my plate to shield my reaction. It had to be the longest two-minute joke I ever heard. As I looked around the table, I could tell that most of the gentlemen, many my close friends, did not know what to do. They too were stunned and embarrassed. After he sat down, there were a couple of polite laughs from others who were just as inebriated. Finally, it was over, or so I thought.

"Anyone else want to tell a joke?" the MC asked. The same guy stood up and told *another* "stupid Ollie with the harelip" joke. One was too many and two was ridiculous. I quietly got up and wandered outside, where I joined a couple of guys having a cigar. I ordered a double Scotch, bummed a cigar, and sat in stunned silence.

People always offer the unsolicited advice "Don't take it personally." Well, that's easy if you're normal. If you're just trying to be normal, then sometimes what people say hurts, whether they're fifty years old or ten years old. Some things never get easy.

CHAPTER 18
Chasing the Pot of Gold

Some kids want to be a fireman, a doctor, or an airline pilot when they grow up. They seem to know what they want to do long before graduating from high school. Stuart knew he wanted to be a lawyer, or thought he knew, until he changed his mind after one year of university and decided to be an actor. I give him full credit for having the guts to change course, even though it was a tough sell to Mom and Dad back home. They cried with disappointment, but years later couldn't be prouder of his decision.

I had no idea what I wanted to be. I was in a corn maze looking for the exit. My lack of career clarity stayed with me right through university. Even after graduating, my entire career was driven as much by opportunity as by design. They say you can be whatever you want, but let's face it: that's not always reality.

I couldn't really ignore the reality of my speech impediment and charge ahead with a career choice, so, in the interest of making a living and not wasting time chasing the impossible dream, I ruled out a few choices early on. My top three non-starter careers were bingo caller, auctioneer, and air traffic controller. Imagine me calling out "N66." Every bingo player needing a number from N56 to G69 would think I'd called his or her number and yell, "BINGO!" Ditto for auctioneering. "Sixty-six hundred dollars! Going once! Going twice! SOLD! To the gentlemen in the third row with the red tie!" Up he'd stand, protesting, "I didn't bid that! You said thirty-three hundred dollars!" An air traffic controller career would have generated nightmares. "Flight six-three-six, you're cleared for landing on runway thirty." The Cessna and the 747 would then both attempt to land on the same runaway at the same time. The outcome would be catastrophic.

Other people in my life thought they knew what I should do better than I did. I took on what the movies call a "non-speaking role." It was the path of least resistance. It was only after I began to have success on *their* chosen path that I was able to walk down *my* chosen path.

I chose my own path when I started my Bachelor of Commerce Degree. My major was marketing and my minor was accounting. My uncle Mac seemed to think accounting was for me! When I was working in the oilfield at a summer job, I was sitting around the office with him and a bunch of guys. I have no idea how my career aspirations came up, but Mac proudly said, "He's going to be an accountant! You should just see him add up a row of numbers!" He was serious. This was his way of saying that I was going somewhere and would be a somebody someday. I remember laughing out loud at his simple connection of adding numbers with my being an accountant. Turns out he was prophetic.

I chose marketing because I was becoming more and more outgoing and had a naïve modus operandi of "What speech impediment?" Ultimately, though, I had to face some facts. The interview with Texaco had been a disaster and I also had an unsuccessful trip to Toronto to interview for a job with a marketing research firm. I realistically concluded that my marketing career needed to be put on hold, at least for the time being.

I interviewed with the Canadian Tax Department for an entry-level tax position and was offered my first full-time job. Things were looking up! Before accepting, I decided to try one other option. I had worked for Ashland Oil in their field operations for three summers, so I thought I would see if I could land a permanent Calgary office job with them. I was confident that I had a reputation of hard work and conscientiousness that would hold me in good stead for a job in the head office, if one existed. So I applied for a job—any job.

David Ravencraft was the Human Resources Manager, an American from Ashland's head office in Kentucky. Unlike the Texaco gentlemen, David was cordial and sincere. He was truly interested in my education and career aspirations. He asked if I'd be interested in a junior entry-level accounting position. A week later came the call with a job offer as a Junior Accounts Payable Clerk for $600 a month ($7,200 a year). There could have been other openings in the company, but even David, with the best of intentions, probably "boxed" me into a certain role. By then, I had come to accept my career fate, at least for the time being.

I then made what would prove to be the first of many career-changing decisions.

Having the opportunity to choose between two job offers is a luxury not afforded to all. Fortunately, many of my career decisions proved to be good ones. I may not have seen the future with perfect clarity, but I had a number of factors on my side: luck (I was in the right place at the right time), sound advice (I had excellent mentors), versatility (I was a jack of all trades), and a solid work ethic (I was a farm boy, remember). In the end, I chose the accounting clerk job over the tax job, even though the tax job paid more. The accounting job wasn't prestigious and I was running the risk of becoming locked into accounting forever, but I guessed it had more upside than toiling for the government. The job started me on a forty-year long career in the oil business.

Being an entry-level invoice clerk (a "checker") in Accounts Payables did not exactly require a university degree. In fact, except for the CFO, who had a university degree and was a CA, I was the only one of about twenty employees in the whole accounting department who had a degree. Some had legitimate non-university designations, such as CGA and RIA, while others simply had bookkeeping courses under their belts.

John Macleod was my first boss, sort of. He was aptly named a "checker" because his job was to check the coding of invoices prepared by others, including mine. Coding invoices involved looking up and writing down codes for the piece of material or service to be paid for, the vendor number, the amount, a brief written description, and numerous other codes that meant something to the computer system, but nothing to me. Coding a couple hundred invoices a day was monotonous. Even a PHD in Mathematics would be prone to errors.

I was a couple of years older than John, but we had a lot in common. A friendship soon developed, along with his wife, Pat, that would last to this day. In fact, I knew Pat was expecting their first child before she did. She was out one night when I was over visiting John. He got the call from the doctor confirming Pat was expecting. Wisely, I knew to leave so they could share the news in private when she got home.

Like all know-it-all, never-satisfied, underpaid, can't-get-ahead-fast-enough new employees, John and I both disliked the department head, our real boss. Not wanting to be an accountant in the first place only fueled the fire. Martin Luther King and I shared something in common. We both had a dream to be free! And all before my first paycheck!

It would have been far better to do my job, stay under the radar, and wait for the right opportunity. Not me! The hunt for something other than accounting started the *morning after the first day*. Not exactly the most politically astute thing to do and it certainly didn't send a signal of commitment to the three layers of authority above me. My efforts to move on were relatively low key the first year or two, but they grew more intense as it became increasingly clear that I was going to be stuck in accounting if I didn't do something about it. It wasn't that I wasn't doing well; in fact, I had been promoted and given raises on a continual basis, advancing to supervisor within two years. But without at least an "A" following my name, like CA, RIA, or CGA, I was going to hit a dead end in accounting. It was only a matter of time.

Like all young adults thriving for complete independence, I couldn't wait until I had a permanent job and got an apartment of my own. I started with Ashland in May 1972 and by the fall I had found an apartment downtown and made the big move from home. With a mix of borrowed furniture and some cheap new basic stuff, I had *my* first home on the twelfth floor of a downtown high-rise apartment. I was making $600 per month before taxes, or about $475 take-home pay. But, with rent at something like $300 a month, I had only $150 to live on. Not much for food, gas, insurance, and the all-important entertainment costs. Butch moved in for a few months while he attended law school, but he couldn't afford to pay much either. It wasn't long before a humbling decision was required; I gave my notice and moved back home with my parents. Fortunately, they were supportive of the idea. So much for stepping out on my own.

My first serious attempt to break out of accounting's Sing Sing prison took place in year three, 1975. An oil scouting position had come open in the land department. I had no clue what an oil scout did, much less what the land department did, but hey, it had to beat accounting! Or so I figured. Scouting is the oil industry's equivalent of a CIA spy. The scout would drive near a competitor's drilling rig and scrutinize the drilling activities. Had they hit a good well or a dry hole? How many feet of drill pipe did they run? Did they run production casing? All this information would prove crucial when making a bid to buy adjacent land for one's own company. All the gathered information was to be communicated to the head office.

Jeep Hall was the Vice President of Land for Ashland. At over six feet tall and weighing over 250 pounds, he must have been a boxer in his previous career. Sonny Liston made only one round against Muhammad Ali; Jeep would have made six. I was still the size of the kid in the corner with the water bucket, but there I was sparring for a job. I listened to him explain, in painstaking detail, how he had worked on the Leduc #1 drilling rig, which was a huge oil discovery in the '40s, and how he had worked his way up to VP Land. Finally, some twenty minutes later, he got around to talking about the job. By then, my mind had drifted and I had forgotten why I was even there. He suddenly asked me why I wanted the job.

"Sir, I worked in the oilfield for three summers, have an

interest in drilling, and, quite frankly, would like a change in career," I answered.

"Well, kid, I think we can do something here. I'll get back to you."

I never got the job despite reliable sources saying that Jeep wanted me. Apparently, the Vice President of Exploration overruled Jeep. Never one to accept no for an answer, even if I was only a lowly accounting clerk, I decided to pay the Vice President of Exploration a little visit. Gutsy or stupid? The answer came back quite tersely. "You'll have trouble communicating with the office over the phone." For a minute, I was tempted to ask if he had ever trained at Texaco, but wisely decided to hold my tongue.

Fate had intervened once again, but this time it was for the good. I soon realized that in my anxiousness to depart accounting, I really had not done my research on the scouting position thoroughly enough. I had allowed my emotions to drive the process. Nothing against scouting; it was an important job. But given my education and long-term ambitions, the job most likely would have been limiting. Nevertheless, my speech impediment was becoming a real pain in the ass.

CHAPTER 19
It's All in the Name

My parents gave me wonderful names, Douglas Hugh, to go along with Gillard. Douglas was a good Scottish name and Hugh after Dad. (Dad was named Hugh after his mother's maiden name, Hughes.) Douglas was always difficult for me to pronounce, so in 1973, after twenty-five years of frustration, I declared to anyone who would listen that I would henceforth go by my middle name Hugh (Hugh Jr. to the local Okotoks crowd). I even sent a memo to all the employees of Ashland about the name change, even though the majority didn't know who I was and didn't care. Hugh wasn't much easier to say than Douglas, but I changed it anyway.

John Macleod, with his typical sense of humour, told me about a fellow at a company he worked at previously who did the same thing. He sent out a memo changing his name from say John Doe to John Smith. No sooner had the memo hit everyone's desks than a second memo came out from a different employee changing his name to John Doe. Fortunately, there was no such smart ass at Ashland.

My last name pronunciation needed some tweaking too. For generations, Gillard has been pronounced "Gill*erd*." Other non-related families pronounced it "Gill*ard*," with the hard "ar" sound. Stuart made the change to a hard "ar" to make it easier for the publicity people in the television and movie business to get it right. His precedent was logical to me. If it was good enough for Stuart, it was good enough for me.

If someone comes up to me and says "Doug Gill*erd*!" then it must be someone who knew me in high school or university days. Like BC and AD, there are Doug and Hugh eras of my life.

A nickname is a term of affection and a stamp of acceptance. Wayne was "Al," after his dad; David was "Ozzie," after his dad; the other Wayne was "Butch;" and Don was "Mouse," for obvious reasons. Mike remained Mike, although his Queens University friends nicknamed him "Cowboy." Maybe because he came from the west? Each time one of us had a new girlfriend, we would introduce everyone by their given names and then call them by their nicknames. The confusion drove them all crazy.

For obscure reasons, my nickname was changed regularly. I had more aliases than a Mafia hitman: "Smokey" after I dropped a burning cigarette between my legs while driving; "Slew" after Seattle Slew, the Triple Crown winner, for how fast I walked; "Silver" after Silver Hill, the local barfly who could knock a tall stack of silver quarters off the table with one swipe of his well-endowed manhood (so the story went). Let the record show that "Silver" was clearly a joke. The gang knew my attributes were quite the opposite of Mr. Hill; a stack of two dimes would have been my limit. The nickname "Gill" stuck the longest, which the guys still use as exclusively their own.

When I was president of an oil company, I once met a Korean business gentlemen by the name of Huygen. His business card showed "Hu" beside his name, perhaps providing a hint on how to pronounce it. When he pronounced his name, it sounded like "Who," which was the same way he pronounced my name. We had a good meeting and promised to meet again.

Some weeks later, the phone rang and the conversation was like a page straight out of the "Who's On First" comedy routine.

"Hello," I answered.

"Hello, who?" the caller said.

"Ah, Hugh Gillard. Who is this?"

"Who," he said again.

"This *is* Hugh," I said, thinking I had heard a question not an answer. "Who is this?"

"Who," he repeated.

"*Hugh*," I replied firmly, ready to hang up. "Who is this?"

After several more "Who" and "Hughs," the caller tried

again.

"This is Hu. From Korea. We met a while ago."

"Oh, sorry. I thought you were asking who I was, Hu!"

We both shared a good laugh. Nothing ever came of the business relationship. I wonder why?

The guy who invented voice recognition for telephone answering should be shot. Well, not literally, but you get the point. The second guy executed should be the executive who decided to replace the corporate receptionist with the voice recognition answering machine. You used to be able to count on the receptionist being a drop dead gorgeous girl with tons of personality. She maybe wasn't on the fast track to becoming the next CEO, but she knew who did what, where to direct your call, and how to make you feel important. Voice recognition does nothing more than recognize what you say, as in "John Doe," and then forward your call to John Doe.

My friend Michel Scott worked for Devon Exploration, one of the hundreds of companies that had switched to a voice receptionist. We hadn't spoken for some time when I decided to call him one day. I was slightly surprised when I had to contend with this new receptionist, who I'll call Miss No-Name. The good news was that I could passably say "Michel," but "Scott" sounded something like "Stot." When I had a cold, it sounded like "Snot."

"Hello, you've reached Devon Exploration. Please state the name of the individual you wish to speak to," Miss No-Name said.

"Michel Stot," I said.

"I cannot make out the name. Please repeat."

"Michel Stot," I said louder this time.

"I'm sorry. Please try again."

"Michel Stot!" Volume is not a good substitute for clarity.

"I'm sorry . . ." Miss No-Name starts in again as I hang up.

If you happen to see Michel, would you mind telling him to give me a call? I've been trying to reach him for years.

CHAPTER 20
Makeover

My ever independent "I am normal" and "I can do this" attitude had helped in achieving some personal goals, but inside I was empty. I never spoke of it to anyone, but the loneliness I felt was wearing thin. I still had not had a date since Connie Lewis in Grade Ten and was still experiencing job rejections over speech. My future, socially and professionally, looked stagnated.

In 1973, I decided I had to make something happen. With the help of my parents, I had worn metal braces for two years and my teeth finally no longer looked like the character Jaws in *The Spy Who Loved Me.* My last operation had been at age twelve, so I thought there surely must be new medical advances to help me further. Could I reduce my lip scar, improve my nose, or even rebuild the cleft palate to improve my speech? My first stop was a plastic surgeon my doctor referred me to.

Talk about the right person at the right place at the right time. Dr. Fowlow was kind, soft-spoken, and had an excellent bedside manner. I had a good feeling about him. He examined me and listened to my questions about plastic surgery advancements. Then, he said, "I would rather be born deaf than with a speech impediment. When people hear you talk, they think you're not intelligent." His body language told me he thought the exact opposite. Finally, someone who understands what living with a speech impediment really means, I thought. Dr. Fowlow was *my* kind of doctor.

I was sent to the local Children's Hospital, even though I was twenty-five years old at the time. The newly created "Cleft Palate Team" concluded that I was a candidate for their services because of my lack of progress on several fronts. The hospital had created this team after determining that clefted children needed a coordinated effort to deal with their multitude of issues. Dentists, orthodontists, plastic surgeons, and speech therapists worked together to offer a full range of skills. I doubt if the concept was unique in the medical field, but to me it was an effective and efficient approach that I never knew existed. A feeling of comfort came over me. Here were people who really cared, who I could talk to, and who could help me.

I jumped at the opportunity to pursue speech therapy. I don't know if speech therapy even existed in the 1950s, but I'm quite certain it didn't exist within 200 miles of where I grew up. But in my late teens, when we lived close to Calgary, then a city of 300,000 people, there likely were speech therapists. For some unexplained reason, neither my parents nor I pursued the idea. It was just as much my fault as theirs. What we didn't know then, I knew now.

My speech therapist's name was Caroline Dunsmore. I haven't seen her in nearly forty years, but I will always be indebted to her. She was in her mid-thirties, pretty, and had a great smile. Maybe we bonded because she was the first to really convince me that I "could speak better if I wanted to," or maybe it was because she too was handicapped. She was in a wheelchair and could use only one hand for reasons we never discussed. It was as if we both knew that we needed to focus on what we could change as opposed to what we could not. We had a lot in common.

Once a week, I made the trek to the hospital to meet her for an hour session. It wasn't long until I started to look forward to it. She would often give me extra time because she insisted that "I get it right" and she genuinely wanted me to improve. We agreed at the outset that I would never speak perfectly, but she inspired me to believe that I could do much better. Caroline never allowed me to say "I can't say it," but at the same time she knew my limits and never set me up for failure. She was a godsend.

Her tool of reinforcement was a tape recorder, the old fashioned reel-to-reel type. It was the first time I had ever heard my voice played back to me. Suddenly, another reality check hit me. I couldn't even understand *myself*! It was nasal and hard to listen to. Many times over the years, friends and associates have said that it took time to get used to how I talked, but once they did they understood me a lot better. It was tough to accept, but hearing myself speak motivated me even more.

Each lesson focused on one set of starting letters. One whole lesson was on learning to say words starting with a "*tr* blend," such as train or truck. It wasn't until I made real progress on one set of words that she would move on to tougher blends, like *ch* and *sh*. On it went, lesson by lesson, letter by letter, word by word. She would often let me take the tape recorder home to practice between lessons, even though it was against the rules. I faithfully tried to perfect the required words or phrases on the recorder. I even tried singing into it once, but readily determined that I shouldn't even sing in the shower.

I lost track of how many lessons we had, but I seem to recall we worked at it for about three years. I was never able to eliminate the nasal sound, but I did make great progress on commencing my words more properly. But as much I learned to *start* the words and enunciate the *middle* parts, I struggled with *finishing* the word. Donald remains Donal. (As I stated earlier, I believe it's because I don't hear the ending of words.)

Caroline's unwavering commitment to make me speak better contributed more than any individual in my life to achieving career and social success, including getting married. This was the new and improved Douglas Gillard!

Within a year of commencing speech therapy, I learned how to say Douglas Gillard, or a reasonable facsimile thereof, but by then it was too late to revert back. The memo had already gone out! Besides, I was proud of going by Hugh, to honour my dad. Friends and family all made a great effort to accept the change, which must have been difficult for them. There is still one uncle who, after forty years, still calls me Doug. I guess some people take longer than others to accept change.

As for Dr. Fowlow, he performed surgery on my bottom and top lips, and partially closed the hole in the roof of my mouth. I took a two week vacation from work and planned it while Mom and Dad were away on a trip so as not to traumatize them. I never even told them I was having the surgery. Only a couple of my best friends, Ozzie and John, knew.

For the bottom lip, Dr. Fowlow made an incision on the inside and cut out a sizeable piece all the way across, thus reducing the lip sag, for lack of a better term, without creating a new scar on the outside. Although it didn't improve my intelligence, it did improve the appearance of intelligence. The top lip was completely re-cut and re-sewn together, but this time in a zigzag fashion instead of a straight vertical line. Dr. Fowlow thought this was not only more presentable, but would also allow a mustache, if I chose, to better fill in and overlap the scar.

It was a good thing I had kept a low profile during recovery. Doctors tend to understate the pain and swelling after surgery—"Just minor pain, nothing serious." Dr. Fowlow's definition of "minor" was not the same as mine. I could have used a self-induced coma to cope. Both my lips were hugely swollen and totally black and blue. The top lip curled up and the bottom one curled down. They closely resembled the rear end of a baboon heading south. I remember Ozzie saying, "No big deal, Gill. It just looks like you were hit by a hockey puck." It killed me to even smile, but I couldn't help but laugh (and cry out in pain at the same time). Ozzie's humour was very healing.

Perfection was not attainable, but the result was dramatic and acceptable. The plastic surgery and the improved speech would form the basis for a whole new social life and career. To top it off, I had actually grown a few inches and filled out a bit since my late teens. The "filling out," once started, continued unabated for twenty-five years, transforming me from a potential jockey to a sumo wrestler. I wasn't the scrawny, underdeveloped kid anymore. There was a new me. In 1974, at twenty-six, I started thinking about dating again for the first time in almost a decade. I had missed out on a lot during my teenage years and early twenties, but it was now time to give dating another try.

CHAPTER 21
Second Date

Although not a candidate for the cover of "GQ," I was ready to ask a girl out. Her name was Ellen and the sister of a close friend. I suppose it was only natural that my first step out in over ten years would be with someone I had known for a while. I would see her often when I visited her brother at his parents' farm.

Ellen was intelligent, charismatic, and, most importantly, single. She had a university degree and a successful career as a social worker. Over the years, I would hang around her parents' place, watching TV, playing pool, or playing cards. She would often come out for the evening and we'd all just sit around and talk. Ellen was part tease and part flirt, so I sensed that if I were to ask her out she would accept.

I asked and she accepted.

Given the momentousness of the occasion—a second date after ten years—you'd think I'd have that night permanently burned into my eternal memory bank. But I don't. We probably went to a movie—nothing too physically awkward or conversationally demanding. It doesn't matter. I fell head over heels for her.

Several weeks had gone by when I convinced her to go

on an overnight camping trip. So much for being subtle! My motives were as obvious as asking her to move to the backseat of a car at a drive-in movie. My anxiousness started as soon as I got to her place. I couldn't pack the car fast enough. I was lucky to even remember the tent. There was only one thing racing through my mind and it was *not* how to set up the tent.

"We'd better hit the road," I said, as if catching a flight rather than driving forty miles to a mountain campground. My '68 Firebird's tachometer was near red line as I pulled away.

To make a long story short, the big event was short—very short. If she thought I was going to hit it out of the ballpark, she was sorely mistaken. I had been thinking all day, years in fact, about my first turn at bat in the big leagues. Alas, I was out of the game before getting to first base.

Later that evening, we had a puff of marijuana that she had brought along. It was the only time I ever tried marijuana. If her objective was to relax me, it worked. I might have hit a blooper single to right field instead of a home run, but I did reach first base. The scoreboard read: Runs 0, Hits 1, Errors 1. All joking aside, everyone remembers his or her *first time,* and I certainly do. So I should! I was twenty-six years old!

I suppose it was inevitable that our relationship would end a few weeks later. Certainly our tryst didn't help matters. I think her words were "I don't want to be a trainer," which I made her repeat since I couldn't believe what I thought I had heard. "A trainer?" I thought. "Really!" I might have been eight to ten years behind, but I was a quick learner! More practice wouldn't necessarily mean perfection, but it would get better. And the practice would be fun.

It was all too little too late.

Like any first-time jilted lover, I was devastated. I had never known what a broken heart felt like, but I sure did now. When I awoke the next morning to go to work, I thought only of her: in the shower, eating breakfast, driving to the office, the entire day of work. Like a typical teenage crush, I struggled with why it happened and wondered whether I would ever date again.

But the genie was now out of the bottle. I was hooked. I anxiously got on with catching up with all the fun I had missed. I began to be more aggressive in asking girls, women by then, to go on dates. I had my heart broken a few times and admittedly broke the hearts of others. It might have been ten years later than it should have been, but I made the most of it. I couldn't catch up fast enough.

CHAPTER 22
Gill Stories III

When I worked at the RCAF Base, the height of the Cold War was raging. Nothing is more real than jet fighters armed with nuclear weapons. These fighters were garaged in a hangar with a high security status and guarded by a ten-foot high chain-link fence with razor wire curled on top. In each of the four corners stood a twenty-foot high guard tower with a twenty-four hour military policeman on duty, armed to the teeth with a high-powered rifle. Any "Ruskie" who dared try and enter this space would be met with force as great as what the fighter jets could deliver.

I was always antsy, so sitting around military barracks in the summer quickly grew boring. I needed things to do. I loved to watch the fighter jets take off and land so it was natural, in my mind at least, to buy a model airplane and fly it in the evenings. The perfect grass space happened to surround the hangar with the nuclear jets.

Flying a model glider on the compound in the evening didn't present a security threat, right? To me, the hangar, razor wire, and armed guards simply meant "stay off." It didn't mean you couldn't walk past.

The first nice evening after dinner, I walked from the

barracks to the grassland, balsa wood plane in hand, to conduct the inaugural test flight. Launching the plane was rather simple: rotate the propeller by hand, twist the elastic behind it until wound up tight, hold the plane at a forty-five degree angle, let go of the propeller, shoot the plane into the sky. My test flight was a success! I ran, with a long overdue smile, to where it landed some fifty feet away.

I thought I heard the words "Halt!" but I continued towards my crashed plane on the ground. "Halt immediately!" barked the voice again, but this time I could tell it came from a tower guard. "Stay where you are! Do not move!"

"Surely this is a joke," I thought. "I'm a dishwasher, not a spy." But the rifle aimed at me was sufficient reason to convince me to stand still. Without turning my head (never give them a reason to shoot!), I could see a Jeep racing towards me with three MPs in it. It was a scene right out of *The Great Escape* with the Nazis screaming up in their Jeep to confront the escapees. They all jumped out as the Jeep screeched to a halt.

"Get down on the ground. Spread your arms and legs out."

I hesitated.

"NOW!" they screamed.

I couldn't have fallen faster to the ground had they shot me in the head, which could well have happened given that all four MPs had their rifles aimed right at it. Then, they stood there, silently, staring down at me. SWAT to them meant "Stand, Watch, and Torment."

Mixed feelings were running through me. I was scared shitless, it's true, but always the naive skeptic, I concluded they must be bored and needed some action. Perhaps they were thinking, "Who cares if the kid wasn't even looking at the hangar? We're going to show the brass that we're ready to meet any security challenge that can be thrown at us. Even if it is the first one ever!"

"The guns probably aren't even loaded," I thought. As they frisked and interrogated me, I worried that this incident might get my brother Irv a reprimand, maybe even throw him out of the force.

"What were you doing out here?" they snapped.

"Ah, just flying a model plane, sir."

After about ten minutes of calling in to their commander and confirming it was not a Cold War incident, they let me get up and told me to go on my way, but not without first warning me to stay away from the area entirely. I slunk back to the barracks, plane in hand. No one needed to tell me twice.

Three nights later, I was ordering a beer at the base bar (even though I was under the legal drinking age). A man dressed in "civvies" was seated next to me.

"So, you survived the other night, I see," he said.

It took a second to register what he was talking about.

"Yes. You know about that?"

"I was one of the MPs." He grinned.

"Really?" I replied. "The guns weren't really loaded, were they?"

"Absolutely!" he said quickly. "We were serious!"

I bought him a beer and thanked him for not shooting me.

In the mid-1980s, I had my first steady job, so it was only a matter of time before I upgraded my car. After the '62 Pontiac, next up was a '68 blue two-door Firebird I bought from my friend John Macleod. It was a great car. I wish I had had enough money to buy my third car without selling the Firebird. It would be a great collector's car today. After the Firebird, I bought cars every two to three years from my brother-in-law Brian Quigley. He leased them through his business and when the primary lease was up, he gave me first chance to buy them at his lease buy-out cost. The second car I bought from him was a two-door Thunderbird. It was a beautiful green with plush green cloth seats, typical of the old-style gas-guzzlers.

Technically, the car wasn't new, but it was new to me. This time I was determined, as all new car owners are for the first month, to keep it clean and perfect. I picked it up on a weekend and announced to friends that "there will be no smoking in this car." This was despite the fact that I smoked, but I figured it might help me cut back on my own bad habit.

Monday morning arrived and I headed for work, wearing a brand new expensive three-piece blue suit. Things were going well. I was proud! About halfway to work, I decided that my self-imposed non-smoking policy was just a temporary measure. I lit one up. Dressed in a new suit, driving a new car with a lit cigarette, I looked like a Mafioso on his way to the next extortion gig. "It doesn't get better than this," I thought.

True, it didn't get better, but it did get a whole lot worse. While sitting at a red light pondering my next move in life, I looked down at the cigarette between my fingers. To my horror, the lit end was gone. One second there was a bright red, glowing end and the next second, nothing. The worst thing for a smoker, next to dying of lung cancer, is to lose the burning end of a cigarette and have no idea where it is. Especially while driving a car. The light turned green and I had no choice but to proceed, all the while anxiously looking for the hot end. If I was lucky, it would be on the floor on the rubber mat. But life had not served me the best of luck so far and clearly this was not going to be the turnaround point. Suddenly, I felt a hot burning sensation in my crotch. I looked down and saw smoke rising up.

In an instant I went from the Godfather to Popeye Doyle (Gene Hackman) in *The French Connection*, weaving in and out of traffic. I clutched the steering wheel with one hand and swiped at my crotch with the other, all the while jumping up off the seat with stiff legs. Finally, I was able to pull over and flick the burning residue off the seat, but not before it had burned a hole in the plush green seat *and* the seat of my brand new suit pants. And that's how I got the temporary nickname Smokey.

One of the perks of my marketing job was travel. After attending an industry conference in Portland, Oregon, my flight back to Calgary was delayed due to bad weather. Several other marketing managers from different oil companies were awaiting the same flight. We had all arrived early, keen to get home. The flight monitor showed a two-hour delay.

What do a bunch of young guys do when their flight is delayed for two hours? They hit the airport pub. What better way to spend your time? It certainly beat the alternative of buying another newspaper and sitting in a hard, non-ergonomic chair designed by some interior designer who had obviously never sat in a chair for more than fifteen minutes.

We told some jokes and spread some industry rumours, all the while consuming the maximum amount of beer that our bladder capacity could handle. More than one trip was made to the men's room to reset the plumbing. No worries. Soon we'd be on the plane and on our way home. At the announced time, we all made our way to the gate number to board. I thought maybe I should make one last trip to the loo just to be sure I could last until after the seatbelt sign went off.

"Naw," I said under my breath. "I can hold it for a half hour."

The loudspeaker finally called us to the gate, but instead of walking directly onto a walkway, we were directed outside and across the tarmac to a small commuter jet plane. My thoughts raced. "What the hell? Maybe there's no bathroom on this plane. Maybe I should run back inside. No, I don't have time. Surely there's a bathroom." Worse yet, it was raining. Running water, in any form, increases my urge to go. I jogged up to the top of the ramp with enough anxiety for three heart attacks.

"Is there a bathroom on the plane?" I immediately asked the attendant.

"No," she said, looking at me as if I had just asked for her first-born child.

Fortunately, the plane wasn't full. I took my window seat midway back and noticed a nice-looking lady sitting alone in the row behind me. No one took the seat beside me and the guys spread out.

Panic was already setting in. "Surely there's a rule against no bathrooms," I thought. I already had to pee and we hadn't even taken off yet. Thus began my flight from hell.

When nature calls at 30,000 feet and there's no bathroom, the options range somewhere between zero and nil, and that's being generous. I tried reading a newspaper to take my mind off it, but it was futile. I would cross and uncross my legs every fifteen seconds with enough groin pain to make kidney stones feel like a minor cramp. After what seemed like an eternity,

I knew that holding out any longer was out of the question. I decided there was little choice but to improvise. As if sent from heaven, there it was staring right at me, tucked into the pocket in front of me. The air sickness bag! A waterproof container!

I instantly devised an emergency plan that was ingenious in its simplicity and could be pulled off without anyone knowing. With the newspaper unfolded on my lap, I proceeded, slowly and without the slightest noise, to "use" the bag. Holding a newspaper, an air sickness bag, and one's plumbing all at the same time presented its own unique challenge, to say the least. Furthermore, to relieve one's self without standing up is a feat in itself and one that requires a lot more of what I didn't have. I couldn't help but think how much easier it would have been if God had been a bit more generous when he granted me my physical attributes. Soon the deed was done without a single passenger knowing, including the nice lady behind me. I folded up the bag like the top of a chip bag and set it down on the floor beside my feet, ready for the final step of the plan. I would take it with me upon landing and dispose of it in the first garbage container I saw. I felt relieved, proud, and embarrassed all at the same time. I settled back for a nice nap.

After finally landing in Calgary, everyone stood up and started pulling down the overhead bins to get their stuff. I reached down for the bag. Horror of all horrors! The top of the bag was intact but the bottom was gone! Void of all substance! I made David Copperfield look like a rank amateur. I guess the bag wasn't waterproof after all. "Damn, where did it go?" I thought. It had drained backwards.

It may have been my overactive imagination, but the nice lady behind me seemed to be struggling to get out of her seat and into the aisle. Her shoes were the problem. They seemed sticky for some unknown reason.

CHAPTER 23
Community Service

Joining the Okotoks Lions Club was my first foray into community affairs. The Lions Club is a tremendous worldwide organization dedicated to making local communities better and with a global mission of helping the blind. I picked it mostly because a lot of the members were my guy friends and that was good enough for me.

Within a couple of years, I was approached to "work my way through the chairs," which is another way of saying they needed a treasurer and then they'd see where it went from there. I was pleased to be asked and so I accepted. Within four years, at age twenty-nine, I was elected President of the Okotoks Lions Club. The position involved running meetings and speaking at banquets. I grew more at ease at the microphone, all the time learning the art of public speaking. I was ignoring my speech impediment. I was who I was. If the audience didn't understand every word, then they could fill in the blanks as they wished. It had been a long road since my Abraham Lincoln public speaking stint in Grade Five, but I was here to stay.

As president of the Okotoks Lions Club, you were also expected to attend other town's Lions Club dinners. Every president always had a member who was also a good friend to ride shotgun with him as he drove to various dinners, often in very poor weather. Ozzie rode shotgun for me all that winter, keeping me company and being my biggest booster when I needed some confidence.

That experience then led to being asked to become a member of the Okotoks Recreation Board, an advisory board to the Town Council, which led to being Chairman in my second year. Whatever I was doing, it was apparent that others felt I was capable of being a leader. After a two-year stint, I stepped down as normal course to ensure new people with fresh ideas would continue to be involved.

Shortly thereafter, I was asked to form a committee of interested town and rural people to look at the feasibility of building a new recreation centre for the town. The town was growing as more and more people migrated from the big city to small towns. Eventually, such moves transform the quaintness of small town living to typical suburbia. But, at the time, the town had no swimming pool and a very old skating and curling rink. We, as the Okotoks Recreation Committee, had the challenging task of determining what type of recreation facility was needed. It required community input, selecting a qualified architect to design the facility, providing input on the design, getting more community input, finalizing the design, and determining the financing options.

One of the valuable lessons I learned both in business and community work is that a leader is only as good as his team.

The overused expression "There is no I in team," is totally true. Over the years, I developed my own effective leadership style, but much of my success was utilizing the team concept, and the Recreation Committee was no different.

The "public face" confidence that I garnered as President of the Lions Club set the groundwork for the many public and town council meetings I attended during the process. Typical of these types of undertakings, there was no shortage of opinions and controversy. The whole process tested my public speaking and negotiating and leadership skills to the limit, but I always had the backing of a superb committee who worked tirelessly on the project.

The only "committee membership" challenge occurred when the town council insisted on appointing a town councillor to the committee to ensure that they always knew what was going on and that we would not "go astray." I was dead opposed to this forced appointment. I had handpicked the entire committee and had total confidence they were up to the job. I did not want the committee to be prematurely or inappropriately swayed by one council rep who would have no real authority, only implied authority. I was determined the committee would evaluate and arrive at the best possible outcome without premature influence of one person saying, "The council will never approve that."

Of equal concern was that I wanted us to be the primary communicator with town council. We would say the right things at the right time and not have the whole process jeopardized because of one individual's personal take on things. The whole experience confirmed to me that standing on principle was the proper thing to do. However, as I was to learn many years later, standing on principle can also have serious career consequences.

By 1981, we had completed our work and presented our final recommendations to council for a vote. The proposed facility involved a skating rink, curling rink, community meeting rooms, and a state of the art swimming pool (the most controversial part). Included with the proposal was a recommended financing structure based on part public fundraising, part rural municipality contribution, and mostly town taxes. After much debate, the town council passed the resolution to borrow the funds and commence the project, provided the committee raised the necessary public funds. I didn't think I should chair the fundraising (since I was living in Calgary at the time, not Okotoks) and asked another member to take over the chairman role.

Years later, a friend said to me that he'd rather donate money to a charity than get involved. To his credit, he was a very benevolent person and supported several charitable causes. I have often thought about what he said. Although contributing is commendable, and miles better than those who are not generous at all, somebody actually has to stand up and do the work or nothing happens.

For me personally, I found it challenging and rewarding to be involved in my community. The Lions Club proved to be just the beginning. Over the years, I got involved in golf club boards and committees, condominium boards, and chaired the Calgary Hospice Society. Most recently, I assumed the chair of the Calgary Zoological Society Board, which provides oversight to one of the finest zoos in North America. I am as proud of my contribution in the not-for-profit areas as the for-profit businesses.

CHAPTER 24
Moving On

After about four years at Ashland, I knew I had to move on. My friend John had left a year earlier to pursue a totally different career and I yearned to do the same. Although I was gaining confidence and performing well (I had been promoted to supervisor, *with my very own office*), I wanted more. Without a degree in accounting, my advancement potential was limited to first-level manager. I had ambition to do better and I knew I could achieve more, even with the speech impediment.

Anyone with a successful career can attribute their success to plenty of factors. You have to have the right people reporting to you and you have to report upwards to the right people. A key factor in my success was that I was *normal* in every way. It wasn't denial, but rather a refusal to accept my speech defect as a deterrent to what I thought I was capable of doing. In my mind, when I spoke, the words came out perfectly. I knew that certain career paths would be more challenging than others, but as far as I was concerned, I simply had to plow ahead if I hoped to achieve something better.

I had one outside job interview while at Ashland, for a position at Dome Petroleum. Dome was a fast-growing, made-in-Canada success story and my friend John Clark was working in the production operations department. He mentioned a new position opening up in accounting that was a liaison-type position coordinating capital spending controls between accounting and operations. It seemed to be more of the same, but the more I thought about it, I determined that the job had two things going for it: it was out of Ashland and it might lead to a career-changing opportunity.

John Clark informed the Human Resources people in Dome that he knew someone who might be interested and would be good at the job (thank you, John!). A few days later, the call came, followed by a couple of interviews, and then a request to be "tested."

"I'm applying for a job in accounting, not the head of the CIA or NASA," I thought. Then, "Would I fail and embarrass myself?" It was, quite simply, put up or shut up time. I agreed to the testing.

Dome had implemented a very unique (for the oil industry, at least) and rigorous screening process on new hires for senior positions. No one was excluded if the position was considered senior enough. The "testing" involved spending a day and a half with a psychological consultant who put you through rigorous written and oral tests, most under very tight time limits, some as little as fifteen minutes. I surmise part of it was to test one's decision making under stress.

The test objectives were, among other things, to assess the candidate's intelligence level, ability to think and reason, communication and people skills, and "best fit" career paths.

From all of this data, combined with the psychologist's observations and recommendations, Dome would decide whether to make a job offer or not. And if you did join Dome, then the testing information and final report would be placed on your personnel file as long as you were an employee. This of course had its pluses and minuses. The problem was that over time, people change. They may well improve on identified weaknesses and grow, but their file remained the same. Ultimately, the test results and reports were removed from the personnel files, which was the proper decision.

When I was invited into the psychologist's office to review my results, you could cut the tension with a knife. He didn't give me the actual report, but did discuss his conclusions. There was no pass or fail—simply a composite of one's skillsets, strengths, and weaknesses. But, in my mind, it was a pass or fail. Either I was good enough to join the company or I wasn't. Simple as that.

"Mr. Gillard, you did very well on the tests," he started out. "You are in the high ninetieth percentile when it comes to intelligence. Career-wise you would make a great lawyer. Regardless, you certainly qualify to be a Dome employee."

I'm not sure why he singled out the law profession for me as I can conjure up good and not so good traits. But the good news to me was I finally had an independent validation of my intellectual abilities. The IQ test I had taken in high school that effectively caused me to split Grade Twelve into two years was bogus. It wasn't that all of a sudden I was brilliant (I wasn't), or that I was better than anybody else (I wasn't), but after spending my entire life trying to dispel the myth that a speech impediment meant lack of intelligence, I finally had the confirmation. Now at least three people knew it: the psychologist, Dr. Fowlow, and me.

The whole psychological testing thing, and thankfully, the results, gave me a badly needed boost in confidence.

In 1977, I joined Dome Petroleum in their newly created accounting position of Supervisor, Capital Control. The title "supervisor" simply gave it some implied authority to the operations staff, as I had no employees reporting to me. This was my first company change ever and something happened that would occur every time I changed companies. I had a sinking feeling that I had just made a huge mistake. Everything was foreign to me: new people, new surroundings, new work.

Compounding my insecurity was that I was creating this job from ground zero. I had to determine the mandate and establish corporate policies for how capital expenditures would be tracked throughout the company. As each month passed, my comfort improved. Years later, I would mentor many people who changed jobs or took big steps up. I assured them that feeling like they had made a mistake is normal and the self-doubt will pass. And it does!

Although the job had no real authority, it had loads of implied authority via the rules I established. Operations were required to funnel their AFEs (Authority for Expenditure) to me. Hundreds of operating staff needed my sign off on their paperwork before going to management for final approval to spend money. This not only gave me profile, but it also came with real responsibility to create and implement sound policies and practices. My higher profile helped me establish a decent reputation throughout the company, which ultimately set the stage for new and bigger things.

The CFO, Vic Zaleschuck, had called me down to his office for a one-on-one meeting. I was nervous. This was the first time he had specifically asked for me, without my bosses.

"We've announced that we bought Siebens Oil and Gas today and have a large pension fund as our partner. The pension fund structure, designed to optimize taxation [code for minimize], is very complicated. Read this summary and tell me what you think of how we should manage and account for it."

Dome Petroleum was on the leading edge of how to grow a company on a tax-effective basis. To greatly oversimplify, Dome spent the capital dollars to maximize its tax write-offs. The value pie had been divided up so that the pension fund got its share of revenue in return for having put up most of the acquisition costs in the first place. Dome balanced this by putting up all future capital costs. Although tax effective, the structure was very complicated to manage and track. It was also difficult to educate all operations people on ownership rules, who paid what costs, and who got what revenue.

The next day, I went back to Vic with my recommendations. I thought that a separate accounting group should be established with three main functions: to determine and monitor the proper processes between land, operations, and accounting; to educate employees; and to act as the liaison with the pension funds. To my surprise he agreed completely. Within a day or two, he promoted me to Manager, Acquisitions Accounting. Once again, I had literally written my own job description. Things were starting to get exciting.

Vic's request kick-started my career success, along with his acceptance of my recommendations, and the subsequent promotion. It sparked a chain of events, including corporate transfers and further promotions, which in turn led to opportunities inside of Dome and beyond.

Besides all of the career positives for me, there was a special bonus. I met and interacted a lot with Glenn Wickerson, the company's tax manager. This was no surprise, given the tax structure of the deals and Glenn's role in creating them. Glenn and I hit it off and developed a friendship that continues to this day, over thirty years later. With our wives, Rosie and Dawn, we have taken countless vacations together. Glenn was one of the brightest and most logical thinkers I ever worked with.

The Siebens deal turned out to be the first of several acquisitions over the next seven years that saw Dome grow several-fold. The next deal was Mesa Petroleum (owned by the famous Boone Pickens of Amarillo, Texas), followed by Sabre, and then Kaiser Petroleum.

By then, Dome Petroleum was the largest independent oil company in Canada. Two competent men ran the company: the chairman, Jack Gallagher, a charismatic and visionary geologist; and Bill Richards, president and CEO, a lawyer by training who was aggressive and growth focused. Between the two of them, the company strived and grew.

Bill Richard's other major attribute was the corporate culture that he created—one that gave employees all the authority they needed, often well beyond industry peers. If you demonstrated an ability to *work hard* and make the sacrifices to *get the job done* and make *good decisions,* you were recognized and rewarded. If you were on the fast track with Dome, there was no limit to your opportunities to flourish. This management style, combined with the company's track record of growth, became very attractive to bright, self-starting individuals. All employees were encouraged (in reality, intimidated) to own Dome shares, which seemed to rise almost daily. Between Bill's drive for growth and Jack's drive for potential Arctic exploration, Dome was on a roll and always searching for the next deal. Everyone was happy.

What goes up must come down. If this weren't true then the tech sector would now be trading in the stratosphere. Oil prices would be $500 per barrel and trees would reach the sky. You see where I'm going with this. The next deal, the biggest, proved to be fatal—the proverbial straw that broke the camel's back.

Dome acquired Hudson's Bay Oil and Gas (HBOG), a large Canadian oil company, owned in large part by Conoco of the US. Secretly, and then by a public offering, Dome ended up with a huge share position in Conoco and then executed a brilliant flanking maneuver. Think country mouse outsmarting the city cat. With such a large position in the parent company, Conoco was all but forced to "trade" the Conoco shares Dome held in return for its HBOG shares. If they refused, they risked losing their entire company to Dome. Strategically, the HBOG acquisition was a good transaction because its huge asset base (largely land rights that the British Crown had granted hundreds of years before) had been managed very conservatively, thus leaving the lands undeveloped and underexploited.

About a year prior to all this, I had been recruited to join the Business Development Department, which I welcomed. My career in accounting at Dome had gone very well, thanks in large part to being in the right place at the right time to help manage the growth. This was my opportunity to move onto something else besides accounting. I sought advice from Vic. He thought it would be a good move for me and offered one piece of advice: "You need to learn not to do everything yourself." This was his way of saying that I needed to learn to delegate better to be a top manager. I never forgot his sage advice and it served me well; in fact, too well. Years later, when working at the most senior executive levels with other companies, I would take the team concept too far, resulting in not necessarily the best decisions being made. Yet, I was ultimately the one accountable. Leadership means making tough and maybe unpopular decisions at times.

So after thirteen years of accounting, I finally had my chance to move into the business side and I jumped at it. Soon, I was given a small takeover deal to "cut my teeth on" and over the next few months I learned a lot about how to do acquisitions. I especially enjoyed working with John Stewart, a truly nice guy and very bright. We became close friends and, even after moving on in our careers, John always gave me sound advice and encouragement. Unfortunately, we rarely see each other these days, but I always look forward to the few times we manage to get together. He remains as positive as ever.

In less than a year of cutting my teeth in Business Development, I was approached to move again, this time to Manager of the Land Administration Department. The job may not sound like much, but it was very challenging. Dome's rapid growth via acquisitions put tremendous strain on various departments and some badly needed leadership. It was risky of me to decline such a promotion, but I knew I'd be locked in again with no way out, like an actor stereotyped in one type of role throughout his career. As flattering and tempting as it was, I declined.

The really good takeaway from all this was that my

confidence continued to improve at a steady pace. Senior executives now looked beyond my speech imperfections and judged me solely on my track record and potential.

Not long after turning down the land position, I was approached to be the executive assistant to John Beddome, then Senior Vice President of Operations. So, after only one year in the M&A department, a job I truly liked, I had a nice dilemma to deal with. The choice was difficult, but with the wise mentoring of some key VPs, I accepted a career change yet again.

From strictly a career perspective, the HBOG acquisition resulted in a new opportunity for me. I was asked to lead the merger of the two organizations, a huge task given that at the time this was the largest merger ever undertaken in the Canadian oil industry. It involved thousands of employees, duplicate operating and administrative divisions, and vastly different management styles. The only order from above was that it was to be a *merger,* not a *takeover*.

This simple policy directive of "merger" proved to be disastrous for the organization. I would never recommend that acquirers mask what is clearly a takeover as a merger of equals. From an organizational perspective, you get the worst outcome. When you try and jam all senior executive and managerial positions together from both companies on an *equal* basis, it is not only highly inefficient, but even worse, many of the best people get frustrated and quit. Dome's best employees hated working for the HBOG executive and vice versa. Management styles were totally different and loyalties ran deep. Consequently, the company lost many of the best people on both sides. It would have been far better to call it what it was—a takeover—and keep the best Dome executive and the best HBOG executive, and then set the organization underneath accordingly.

Despite the successful integration, excluding the people issues caused by the flawed policy, the new and bigger Dome Petroleum was ready to continue to grow and prosper. But, a new and bigger issue loomed on the corporate horizon that soon became all consuming. Oil prices started to collapse and interest rates on the company's large debt were rising along with inflation. People were taking bets on when oil prices and interest rates would cross. An unimaginable event today, but a plausible outcome back then. Interest rates ultimately rose to as high as seventeen percent and oil prices declined to the low $20 per barrel.

The HBOG deal came with a lot of debt, debt that was on top of the debt the company already incurred from previous acquisitions. It did not take a PhD in Mathematics to see that Dome was heading for disaster if something wasn't done, and done soon. Fortunately, the stock market still saw the company as a darling with the share price hovering around an all-time high in the mid-$20 range (after several share splits), largely on the hype of the potential drilling success in the Beaufort

Sea. There was only one solution: issue equity to pay down the debt while there was still a demand for Dome shares. In the business it's called "taking the money when it's there."

To make a long story short, Jack and Bill could not bring themselves to issue equity (perceived to be dilutive to the shareholders), despite pleas from senior financial executives in the company to do so. They believed Dome was too big to fail, or better put, too big for the banks to put under. They could not have been more wrong. Oil prices did not recover and a slow death by a thousand cuts began. A good company and thousands of employee savings, including mine, were to be ruined. There were no pensions for many who had spent years building the company and doing their jobs.

In time, a new board (which the banks heavily influenced) gave the exit to certain Dome executives, including Jack and Bill. A new CEO, Howard MacDonald, from Scotland, was hired to fix or sell the company at any price. Employee concerns were the least of his. No other solution existed, except to be taken over. Amoco, then a huge international company out of Chicago, was the successful suitor. In 1984, Dome ceased to exist. The rise and fall of Dome supposedly became a Harvard Business School study case—no doubt illustrating how either one big deal mistake or not issuing badly needed equity when it has an opportunity to do so can cause a company's demise.

During the turbulent years prior to Amoco's takeover (it was not a merger!), my career had peaked. Being on the fast track of a company going nowhere was of little value to me. I spent some time in specific jobs in operations and land, but I was clearly in no man's land with my career. Despite having been promoted several times with a proven track record, I didn't receive a single phone call from any executive search agency, or headhunters. Maybe it was because I was a "jack of all trades" as opposed to an expert in accounting, geology, or engineering, but I suspected it had more to do with my speech impediment than anything else. While most my capable Dome friends were getting calls and leaving for new challenges elsewhere, I was staying put. In fact, in my entire career, I only ever received one phone call from a headhunter and that was some fifteen years later. But that's another story.

However, my fortunes were soon to change. Two years before the Amoco takeover, an opening showed up in the Dome Natural Gas Marketing Department for a Regional Marketer. It wasn't a management role, but it was in marketing. Here was a chance to do what I had always wanted to do since the disastrous Texaco interview back in 1972. Flawed speech and all, I was given a chance to be a marketer and will always be indebted to my friend Rick Funk for recommending me for the job.

The Canadian natural gas market was then in transition from regulated sales and pricing to a free market. It was an exciting time to be on the leading edge. Dome may have lost much of its industry influence as it struggled to survive financially, but it still had a lot of talented people willing to take risks and lead the way in pursuing new business opportunities.

Gas marketing in a non-regulated environment was a perfect fit for Dome. We had the excess un-contracted gas to sell and the gas utilities were beginning to look at buying their gas needs directly from the producers rather than the pipelines that, until then, had a monopoly on gas sales. The pipelines would ultimately become purely the transporters and not the wholesalers or middlemen.

It was my first taste of marketing and I loved it. Cold calls, building customer relationships, understanding their needs, setting marketing strategies—the whole nine yards. Travelling to various cities in my marketing region—the Pacific Northwest—and making cold calls was a bit unnerving at first, and actually never got easy. However, we had lots of product to sell, the size to stand behind future commitment, and we were one of the first to enter the deregulated market fray. My predecessor had already initiated some of the contacts, but there was still a lot of work to be done to get a deal across the line. Two years later, I was pleased to close the first ever long-term sale of British Columbia natural gas out of Canada. It was a ten-year deal to Washington Natural of Seattle.

Finally, after fifteen years, I had a clear career path ahead of me. One that I not only liked, but also could excel at, and *in marketing,* of all things!

The Amoco takeover was, as expected, a real clash of culture. The companies could not have been more different. There were a lot of very good people in Amoco, but it had developed a huge bureaucratic culture. Decisions, even the mundane, took several meetings, sometimes trips to the head office in Chicago, and too much time. Worst of all, their willingness to take risks lay somewhere between money under a mattress and government bonds, so we lost deals that should never have been lost. It was incredibly frustrating. Dome had not been perfect by any means (as evidenced by certain executive decisions that led to its demise), but it still had innovative people who could lead in a changing marketplace. Amoco had been a successful company, but had lost its entrepreneurial spirit with size and bureaucracy.

So, the inevitable was bound to happen. It was time to move on.

CHAPTER 25
The Last "First" Date

I was early, way too early. It was way earlier than the social standard of being just a touch late so as to not appear overly anxious. So, ever so slowly, at near stalling speed, I drove around the block. It seemed to knock only seconds off the clock. I drove around the block again and then once more for good measure. Finally, it was two minutes after seven and so I parked in front of the house. I had gone from having never been in the neighbourhood to now being qualified to give guided tours.

It was a blind date and her name was Rosemary. I knew nothing about her. I nervously walked up the steps to her house, wondering if she had peeked out her curtains to see me first. If she did, she must have wondered why I was circling like some stalker. The moment of no return was the ringing of the doorbell. For better or worse, the blind date was on.

"Hi," we said in unison as she opened the door. If she was as nervous as I was, she hid it well. Her disarming smile was the first thing that struck me. She was small and cute and looked stunning in a purple dress.

"Come on in for a second," she said. "I just need to check on something before we go." I followed her to the bathroom. A man on all fours was trying to fix the plumbing. "Hugh, this is my ex-husband, Jim. Jim, meet Hugh."

The Idiot's Guide to Blind Dating had no section on how best to react when meeting the other person's ex-spouse on the floor of a bathroom. It was an author's oversight, for sure. We were both stunned to see the other and the best we could each come up with was to grunt "Hello." Questions raced through my mind. "Does he still live here? Is he a plumber? What have I gotten myself into?" As awkward as it was for me, I could only imagine what he felt like sitting on a bathroom floor looking up at some skinny guy about to go out with his ex-wife.

"And there's someone else I'd like you to meet," she said. "These are my daughters, Heather and Tracey. Say hi to Hugh, girls." My, the surprises never end. In less than five minutes, I had gone from being the nervous half of a blind date to meeting an entire family, including an ex. "Surely, it can only get better from here," I thought.

Mutual friends of ours had arranged the blind date. Mike Stewart was a good friend. He and I had spent countless evenings together going out to bars and nightclubs, and the occasional dinner, playing the field looking for girls. We were both in our thirties and he had been dating Marilyn for a long time and I came to know her well. Marilyn's good friend was Rosemary Feeney, the divorced lady with two kids. They jointly concluded that we would be a good fit for each other and the blind date was conceived.

Both of us were asked some days in advance if we'd be

interested in a dinner out at Mike's favourite Italian restaurant, La Picolla. Trusting our mutual friends' judgement of character, we both said yes. "No harm in trying," I thought, "and who knows, it might just work." Either by simple oversight or intentionally waiting until it was too late, a minor but important detail had been overlooked. At three o'clock on the day of the big date, we each received a phone call from Marilyn.

"Hugh, I thought I better mention something. Rosemary hates smoke."

"Rosemary, I forgot to tell you that Hugh smokes."

This little bit of surprise information was the equivalent of the radio operator telling the Titanic captain, "Iceberg fifty feet ahead!" A bit late, but Rosemary must have concluded the same as I did. It'll probably go nowhere for sure now, but it's too late to cancel.

The dinner went fine, despite my failed attempt at masking that I smoked by holding the cigarettes down and around my chair between quick puffs. We ate and drank, then went to a nightclub to dance and drink some more. Finally, it was time to end the evening and take her home. As I was about to walk her to her front door, my mind was cluttered with nervous indecision. How does one say goodnight to a divorcee? Do I kiss her or just say thanks and goodbye? Torn between two choices, with time elapsing, I split the difference.

"Thanks for the evening. It was fun," I said and then impulsively shook her hand. Shook her hand! What was I thinking? What did she think? "Maybe he's gay. I've never had a guy shake my hand before." The odds of the evening being a one-time only event had just increased exponentially.

Besides my affinity for smoking and her hating even the thought of smoking, we were much different in other ways as well. I was single and so I thought and planned ahead like a single person. She, on the other hand, was a single mother working at a bank and raising two daughters. Maybe it was because she was so different from me, but I was smitten! After a few days to get up enough nerve, I called her to see if she'd be interested in going out again—that night! It had escaped me that as a single mother with two kids at home she might need to plan ahead. Despite yet another faux pas, she said yes, but it would have to be a different night, a week away. This relationship might have legs, I decided!

CHAPTER 26

CanWest

Mike Stewart was also on the Board of Directors of CanWest Gas Marketing Company. CanWest was a company born out of the privatization of a government-run department controlling natural gas transactions in British Columbia to being owned by BC gas producers, who in turn owned the underlying gas supply. It was all part of the deregulation process.

The fledgling private company needed to build a team of marketers to develop new markets and a supply team to acquire the gas and build relationships with producers. The Vice President of Supply position was still open and Mike asked if I'd be interested. He felt that with my many years of working for a producer, combined with my marketing skills and knowledge, I'd be a good fit. Besides, he knew that I really wanted out of Amoco. I want to go on official record as saying that the door Mike opened for me truly changed my career and life and I will be forever grateful to him. Without Mike's willingness to stick his neck out for me, who knows where my career would have gone. He is one of the smartest, most generous and loyal friends I have.

Once again, it was all about being in the right place at

the right time. The CEO concurred that I would be a good fit (speech impediment and all). I will always appreciate him taking a chance on me. So, in 1990, after thirteen years with Dome and Amoco, I left to join CanWest as VP Gas Supply.

CanWest's head office was in Vancouver, but the supply department would be located in Calgary, near all the oil and gas producers. What supply department? There was no office or people. I once again worried that I had made a big mistake, a pattern I was developing each time I left the comfort of a familiar job for the great unknown of a new job. "This is what you wanted, so there's no going back now," I counselled myself. I didn't know where to start.

I am proud to say that within a few months, with the help of Bruna Martinuzzi, our Human Resources Manager at the head office in Vancouver, a new CanWest Gas Supply Department was born and open for business in Calgary. An office, furniture, staff, strategies, policies, and processes were all put in place from scratch. For us, competing for new gas supply was as much about marketing to buy gas as it was for the Vancouver marketing department selling it. Both departments required the same skills. Each day presented a multitude of new challenges to deal with. About six months later, the President and CEO, said to me, "You need to operate more like a Vice President." He wasn't referring to how I managed downward, but rather upward. In my effort to communicate upward, I was, in effect, asking for permission to do things when I should have been proceeding on my own. He was correct and his small bit of feedback made me a better executive.

I will always be proud of our team who stepped up and got the job done. In my biased view, they were the best gas supply department of any gas marketer in the business. One never really knows how you are perceived when you head a group of people, but I believe I developed a culture that was always positive, despite some real challenges. Loyalty is earned, not bought. Success without loyalty is rare.

It had now been some twenty years since the Texaco interviewers told me "There's no way you'll make it as a marketer with the way you talk." I was now the vice president of a natural gas *marketing* company.

Ironically, as it turned out, one of the larger producers in the CanWest supply pool was Texaco. They needed to create a spinoff company holding leftover Canadian assets. But, a serious barrier stood in their way: they needed CanWest's (my) approval to reassign the gas contracts to the new entity and proceed with the asset spinoff.

Two Texaco gentlemen, Greg Romney, Senior VP, and Tim Pritchard, VP Marketing, paid me a visit. Over the next couple of weeks, we met several times to negotiate an agreement that would be a win-win for both sides (a fundamental negotiating principle of mine). I could not help but think of the great irony of this. After, and *only after,* we signed the deal, I mentioned my not-so-good experience with some of their head office personnel. They of course knew nothing of my history with Texaco and I could tell they were relieved that I hadn't held a grudge. Greg and Tim were both of solid character and would shortly be promoted to president and vice-president of their company, respectively, and we maintained a very cordial yet business-like relationship.

When Tim retired a couple of years later, I attended his retirement party, along with several dozen other industry executives. In his farewell speech, he said the usual niceties about his staff, coworkers, and friends in the business, and then he said, "And I want to especially acknowledge Hugh Gillard, standing there in the back. Thanks, Hugh, for not holding things against us." No one in the crowd knew why he said it or what he meant, but I knew! I silently nodded, acknowledging my appreciation for his comment. He was a class act. I knew that a unique chapter in my life, spanning over two decades, had finally closed.

The CEO of CanWest had a very difficult role. He had to set strategy for what was essentially a new company with very demanding shareholders—the producers who provided the natural gas supplies. In the age of decreasing regulation and evolving free markets, the producers, in particular their own marketing departments, were both suppliers and competitors.

In many ways, CanWest was in a no-win situation from the start. It would only survive if it took more risk on behalf of all producer suppliers than the producers would take themselves, *and if* the risk paid off with better than market prices. There was lot of gas supply trapped in BC with limited pipe transportation to distant markets such as the US Pacific Northwest and California. With our largest shareholders giving a verbal nod of the head, the CEO stepped up and made huge long-term pipeline commitments; in essence, mortgaging the company. The pipeline commitments could only be met if gas prices were better than what the producers could get directly on their own volition and they continued to supply new gas to CanWest. Simply put, if the gamble didn't pay off, the supply would dry up and CanWest would be in serious trouble.

For three years, things went well for the company. New markets were developed along with new supplies, but, the US pipeline expansions were nearing completion and CanWest's obligation to pay the costs kicked in; in other words, CanWest needed to pay off multiple mortgages of fifteen to twenty years. But, overregulation had glutted the natural gas supply in North America and, when all that gas hit the market, prices soon collapsed. A dream come true for the buyers, but to suppliers like CanWest, who held the very expensive pipeline capacity, low prices were disastrous.

With non-competitive prices being paid back to producers, one did not need a PhD in Economics to see trouble on the horizon. The tsunami blame game hit fast and hard. The CEO took tremendous heat from our producers, all of whom had 20/20 hindsight. Compounding his problem was the fact that none of the producers' approvals had been formalized to take on the pipeline contracts. Soon, they were reneging everywhere, arguing that they had never said yes in the first place.

Not helping matters was his style. He was a very smart man, but he did not react well when challenged by shareholders. When the producers, the company's lifeblood, challenged him he pushed back to the point where it all became personal. On the other hand, I had developed a solid relationship with the producers and soon found myself caught in the middle. Making matters worse, he and I disagreed on how best to deal with our largest supplier who was the most vulnerable to the long-term pipeline payment deficits. They were not only the largest supplier, but also their supply contract made them so committed to CanWest that they would likely be the last one standing and left holding all the bills. Not surprisingly, they wanted out so badly they threatened to sue us over technicalities.

I'm sure the CEO thinks that I wasn't loyal to him, but I can truly state that I didn't agree with many of the producers who tried to blame him for the commitments made on their behalf. When it didn't work out for CanWest, they wanted out, and at no cost to them. I, however, disagreed with his confrontational style of blaming the producers.

As time went on, producers could see the split in the executive team. It all came to a head when some key producers banded together and put pressure on the Board to change leadership. Ironically, it was the Texaco executives, as a major shareholder, who lobbied other shareholders that I become President and CEO.

Ted Best was the Chairman of the Board of Directors, a true gentleman who was well respected in the industry. It was his uneviable responsibility, along with the entire Board, to determine the best course of action. Only recently did he reveal to me that when he called several shareholders about the possibility of appointing me President a couple of them expressed conerns about "Hugh's speech impediment." Ted response was, "that has absolutely no relevance to our decisions." Without people like Ted in the business world, I would not have succeeded.

A little over twenty years after being told I would "never make it in marketing because of my speech," I was appointed President and CEO of a marketing company.

I was having dinner at an Italian restaurant in downtown Vancouver the night before the decision was to be announced. As I sat there sipping a glass of red wine and waiting for my order of veal pizziola, I had time to reflect on my first day in Grade Two and everything in between.

There are many cleft afflicted people who, to their immense credit, have achieved great success: Peyton Manning, Jesse Jackson, Stacy Keach, and Joaquin Phoenix. I also greatly admire Lee Raymond, a man with a cleft lip who became CEO of Exxon Mobil. When I heard him testify in front of Congress, he spoke perfect English. Me, not so much! This group of men must have had only a cleft lip or the best palate surgery ever, for I understand every word they say. Nevertheless, they overcame what must have been tough challenges. I may not be in their category of success, but I'm proud of what I've achieved having a cleft lip *and* cleft palate. In all my years in business, I never encountered a CEO who had both.

If I had been given the choice between a cleft lip and a cleft palate, I'd take the lip every time. Yes, a cleft lip is socially traumatic, but with surgery and the maturing of society in dealing with physical defects, it isn't the end of the world. A cleft palate, though, stays with you forever. Although speech can be improved and maybe even perfected nowadays, it presents a real challenge to live with.

My speech, which had improved greatly, was still far from clear. Fortunately, all those who influenced my career along the way focused not on my deficiencies but on my abilities. CanWest was relatively small by international standards, but still in the Top Ten of North American gas marketing companies. From my biased perspective, it was a major achievement.

Shortly before I was promoted to President and CEO, my dad passed away. I believe in his heart that Dad was proud of what I had achieved in my career and in life. I just wish he had lived to see this accomplishment.

He died of prostate and bone cancer after months of severe pain. I never appreciated until after he passed away just how close we were. Even though he never offered the emotional support that I felt I needed, I was always proud of my dad. To me, he was the Alan Ladd character in the movie *Shane*—the quiet, solid, dependable cowboy who stood up for what was right. Mom, Jean, Brian, Rosie, and I took turns sitting with him 24/7. Irv and Elaine joined the vigil with a few days to go and, fortunately, Stuart made it back from California in time to say goodbye.

Maybe it was the culture we grew up in, our conservatism, or maybe the remnants of the Victorian era, but I don't recall our parents saying they loved us or showing physical affection. There was no doubt we were loved, as evidenced by how we were raised, but they never expressed it. People just didn't say it back then.

As Dad lay dying in the hospital, Rosie pulled me aside and asked, "Have you ever told your dad you love him?" I wanted to say yes because I knew that to be the proper answer, but in my heart I knew better and told her no. "You should before he goes," she firmly encouraged. Not much later, it was my turn to sit with him, alone and in silent vigil. It was one of the hardest things I ever did, but I held his hand and said, "I love you, Dad." He hadn't spoken for days and was nearly comatose, but somehow I know he heard me. And saying it made me a better and more fulfilled person. He died later that night.

Usually, when a new leader takes over, a short honeymoon period ensues when he is allowed some time to assess the situation and establish a new strategic direction. Just how long a time is tricky: too much shows lack of leadership and too little may show an impulsive management style. Change at the top is traumatic for all employees, especially those who are loyal, sometimes blindly, to the previous president. Change at the top leads to initiated and un-initiated changes, some healthy and necessary and others exacerbating the already high stress. My honeymoon period lasted all of one day. There were serious problems, both organizationally and competitively, that needed to be dealt with quickly.

The first thing you learn as a president is that there is no one in the organization you can talk to! They all either work for you or are on your board or are shareholders. The job of president, even for a grocery store, is like no other. People outside the company are either competitors or not familiar with the issues. It is, as they say, very lonely at the top. I consumed much of my quiet time in the early mornings and late evenings, thinking my way through the many personal, organizational, and strategic challenges to arrive at appropriate decisions.

To list all the problems the company had in the head office, particularly in marketing, would render this book a management manual, which it is not. In general, I felt that some key senior head office people didn't take enough responsibility in recognizing our lack of competiveness and the urgency to find solutions. To oversimplify, they thought the gas supply simply showed up in Calgary and would always be there. It was akin to the small neighbourhood grocery store proprietor thinking he could sell his lettuce at twice the price of Safeway's next door and never lose customers. If he didn't figure out pretty quickly what products would keep his customers loyal and change his store business model, he would soon be out of business. Customer loyalty only goes so far.

Ted Best called all of the head office employees together to announce the change at the top. Ted explained the Board's decision and indicated its total support for me as the new President and CEO. I then gave a short but sincere speech about "having a great team" and "having great opportunities." I also touched briefly on the need for change, particularly in accepting responsibilities. I was trying to set the tone that as a company we must focus on improving our competitiveness. I was referring to the pipeline capacity mostly, which, if not solved, would eventually strangle the company to death. Some people received it well and others didn't, particularly those who were loyal to the previous president.

Over the next four years, I commuted from Calgary to Vancouver each week. Not surprisingly, some employees quit and some had to be released, including vice-presidents. I had to focus on reducing liabilities to give us any chance at all of survival. To build loyalty I met with the employees and asked them how CanWest could do better. It was my way of showing them they had a stake in the company and that their opinions mattered.

As I commented earlier, being CEO is a very lonely job, and I would be lying if I said the whispering and nickname of "Captain Axe" was not unsettling, but I stayed the course. Over the next four years, we reduced our pipeline commitments by over $60 million, which gave us options for the future.

The most successful presidents are those who understand the competition and can see where the business is headed. But, there is no book with all the answers. My key role, with input from senior staff, was to figure this out and set a course for the future. Setting the course was incredibly challenging because the natural gas marketing business was changing every day with deregulation in Canada and the US. Companies like Enron were writing the book on energy trading and creating new tools in the marketplace that CanWest simply couldn't offer. No one knew at the time that Enron would eventually implode on itself with corruption and fake financials. At the time, they were formidable competitors. A company needs a balance sheet (or deep pockets to handle the massive credit risk involved) if they want to buy and sell gas in a deregulated market and offer customers total flexibility in pricing and delivery terms. CanWest did not have a balance sheet per se, as it was a flow-through business model. To oversimplify, we sold gas and flowed the net after costs revenue directly back to the producers like a giant co-op.

For a positive outcome (on behalf of our producers), CanWest needed to create some "sale value," consolidate with other Canadian competitors like us, and get more efficient. This meant we had to relocate the head office to Calgary, where all the other competitors were. I couldn't announce this strategy—which proved to be correct—to staff or others without the support of the Vancouver VPs. Their support was necessary in order to retain key employees. Some of them didn't support the relocation, so a very difficult decision was made to sever ties.

Terminating people, especially close associates, is a very unsettling process. It doesn't matter how generous you are, the process is always painful and invariably turns friends into enemies. Unfortunately, I became a bit of an expert on terminating people, a job attribute no one wants, and learned the hard way on how best to do it. I learned that it is far better for all parties to make the exit quick and clean. On at least two occasions, I offered a graceful exit and true retirement over time, along with a generous severance package. Despite my intentions to ease the transition, these situations always backfired. The individuals never accepted the genuineness of the offer and were highly critical of the company and me during the transition period. A lose-lose situation.

Ultimately, CanWest was relocated to Calgary. Those who didn't move were replaced. These were tough decisions, to be sure, but the correct ones. A whole new company culture was created and, to this day, I still hear from past Calgary employees who say the new CanWest corporate culture was the best they had ever experienced in their careers. It still makes me proud to hear it.

As per the strategy, I began initiating high-level conversations about potential mergers with like-competitors who faced the same challenges we did. The ideal personal outcome for a CEO is to stay on as CEO along with your key management and staff. I had developed a reputation (I think) of looking after shareholders' interests first, so I established the tone early that we must do whatever was best for the company, and "who runs it" is secondary.

Serious discussions with a potential merger candidate were well underway when I got the phone call that would change my life. For the first time, I got a call from an executive search agency. Friends in the business, some who were less qualified than me, had gotten these calls for years to consider changing jobs, but I had not. They wanted to know if I would consider being President and Chief Operating Officer of a medium-sized oil and gas company. The timing would have been ideal a year later, but I knew that type of opportunity doesn't come along very often. After handpicking a capable interim CEO who was put in place to see the merger through, I moved on to an energy trust as President and COO.

CHAPTER 27
Gill Stories IV

As Vice President of Supply with a natural gas marketing company, one of my responsibilities was to keep on top of government regulations and the people who oversee such policies. One such key regulatory board was the National Energy Board (NEB), who considered applications to export natural gas. It was in our interest to keep in touch with certain Board members, so Brian Hodgins, Vice President of Marketing, and I decided to take one of the members, Byron Horner, out for a round of golf and lunch. It was all about schmoozing and convincing him that we were good and competent people in the business. Byron loved to be entertained.

After our round of golf, it was time to freshen up and head to the clubhouse lounge for drinks and lunch. Byron had enjoyed the round of golf and looked forward to some chit-chat time. Brian and Byron took seats beside each other at the table and I took one directly across. We all ordered a drink. I can't remember what they ordered, but my drink of choice was the Mexican beer, Corona. Up to this point everything was going well.

Corona beer is normally served with a lime wedge that can either be squeezed into the bottle or pushed down inside. I chose, rather routinely, to push mine in. I remembered seeing someone once put his thumb on the top of the bottle and tip it upside down so the lime wedge would better mix up in the beer. I think the proper method was to tip the bottle over once, then back up, release the thumb, and enjoy! If anyone could screw it up, I could. I either tipped it over more than once or shook it a bit too much because the Corona instantly turned into the equivalent of a seltzer bottle.

Foam sprayed everywhere! I tried to keep my thumb on the top to stop the spraying, but that caused more pressure and only made it worse. I was like a little kid at the end of a fire hose. The beer sprayed in every direction, including all over our esteemed guest. I interpreted the look on his face as "Forget about any export permits. Idiots don't qualify." Fortunately, he had a good sense of humour though and we all shared a good laugh.

When I first met Rosemary, she asked if I liked downhill skiing. She and her two daughters loved to ski. In the interest of making sure I stayed in the dating game, I said, "Yeah, I love skiing!" As if I was a natural and did it all the time. I had skied maybe four times in my life and had just graduated from the bunny lift to the green chair. Moguls were cliffs as far as I was concerned. I hated skiing and figured it was a sure way to die.

I never had a good sense of balance in skiing. I had once

lost my balance and fell on top of a young kid's skis. I was embarrassed enough laying there with my legs straight up in the air, but then the wet-nosed six-year-old screamed, "Don't you know you're supposed to ski in control?" That was the worst. Whatever happened to respect for adults?

Another rather embarrassing time, at a different ski hill, I entered a chairlift line that resembled an automated food-packaging line. Skiers fed into the empty chairs like chocolate bars merging into the wrapping process. Everything was perfectly synced and non-stop. One hiccup and the whole system would grind to a halt. Skiers got onto the lift inside a small building where the lift operator stood in a pit up to his waist, one hand on the controls and one hand pushing down the safety bar once the incoming chair had been loaded. An empty chair comes around, one or two skiers get in front in perfect time to sit on the chair, and the operator lowered the safety bar. Off they'd go, heading up the hill. Five seconds later, another fill-the-chair routine.

I entered the moving alternating chair line too fast. Should I take this chair? The next one? I felt the same horror when I hit the tank stand with the trailer. I was going too fast and heading for a disaster. In a nanosecond, I missed *my* chair and veered off to the right, heading toward the operator standing in the pit. His face is forever etched in my mind. He saw me coming at him full speed and froze in sheer terror, probably thinking, "Do I shut off the chairlift or jump?" He chose wisely, jumping up and out of the pit, which was no mean feat from a standing position. Into the pit I roared, like some out-of-control car veering off the street in a police chase. I flipped straight up in the air and landed on my back in the bottom of the pit. The only thing visible to the skiers coming from behind were two skis sticking out of the pit horizontally, like road kill. In the true spirit of capitalism, the chairlift never stopped, lest it cost the ski operator a couple of dollars. Skiers behind me never ceased getting on the lift, but not without first looking down at the idiot lying in the pit unable to get upright. I was so embarrassed I considered staying down there until dark.

Mike Stewart and I have been close friends for almost forty years. Although he was from Okotoks, our friendship began in earnest after we both graduated from university and started our careers in the oil and gas industry. I am also the proud godfather of his oldest son, Brendan, so we're connected at the hip, so to speak.

Our childhood years could not have been more different. I grew up on a ranch and Mike grew up in a small town. Mike's grandfather had a ranch many years before Mike was born, so unbeknownst to me, he had a secret hankering to return to his roots. Eventually, while at the peak of a very successful career, he purchased a mid-size ranch in the beautiful foothills of Alberta, southwest of Calgary. The irony never escaped me that he grew up in town and ended up on a ranch, while I grew up on a ranch and ended up in town.

Besides using the ranch for pleasure and, hopefully making a profit, he also used the ranch for special marketing opportunities, including having staff and special guests out for a trail ride and barbeque. It was at one such occasion that the tale of a "Horse Called Asshole" was born.

Of the thirty invited guests and spouses, there was likely only one person who had spent any time on a horse. Me. Maybe a dozen people knew the difference between a horse and a donkey. The rest were diehard city folks who had never stepped on a farm, much less been on a horse. Mike had his own horses, including a palomino, but for this occasion he needed to rent some trail horses for the day. Announcing that the horses had been rented from a former champion bronc rider in the Calgary Stampede was probably too much information. It only served to heighten the nervousness and jitters of those who had never been on a horse before. In western lore, they were known as "tenderfoots."

At one end of the corral stood the rented horses, saddled and ready. At the other end stood twenty-nine nervous tenderfoots, each wondering which horse they would get. Would it be the mean-looking black one or the one pacing nervously as if never ridden before? I'm sure the majority hoped for the sleepy-looking horse. No one spoke a word. They were probably too busy praying. Or felt like condemned men waiting for execution. No one wanted to be accused of being chicken, but clearly some were wishing they could return to the bar at the house.

Don, the ranch foreman, brought over the palomino for Mike to ride. Just as he finished tying him up to the rail, something caused the horse to panic. He reared back, front legs kicking out, pulling hard on the reins to get free. The reins snapped and the palomino bolted away, saddled and all.

"Get back here, asshole!" Don yelled at the horse, to no avail. Aghast, the trail riders watched without uttering a word. Then, out of the back row of the crowd, a meek yet clear female voice said, "I hope I don't get Asshole." Everyone roared with laughter. The tension was broken. And yes, no one got Asshole.

Airport security has had screening machines for decades, but now we have body pat downs or full body scans for those who get their kicks having their body go viral on the Internet. Rosie and I have been through countless security checks. Most were routine, but not all.

On one vacation to the US, Rosie, in her infinite wisdom, purchased a handheld massage machine to bring home. This "machine" was about two feet long and comprised of mostly metal and hard plastic. One end contained battery-activated rollers that were turned on by a switch further down the handle. The other end was wrapped in leather, for better grip, I assume. Supposedly, you would turn the massager on, hold one end with one hand, and press down the rotating rollers with the other to get the "best massage ever," at least according to Rosie.

I chided her for buying it because I knew she'd never use it when we got home. They were available in Canada and it would take up badly needed luggage space. "Hey, don't worry about it!" she snapped. "I'll just put it in my carry-on bag and it won't bother you a bit."

It was time to head to the airport, bags packed and ready. With total predictability, Rosie announced that her carry-on bag was full, so would I mind if she put the machine in *my* luggage? Minutes became hours as we waited to checkout of our hotel, waited in traffic driving to the airport, waited to drop off the rental car, waited for the shuttle to the terminal, waited to check in, and (wait for it!) waited at security. By this time, I had waited so long and so often I could have taken a stagecoach home quicker.

Finally, it was our turn to go through security screening. Rosie went first with me behind her. The routine is now so routine that everyone turns into human robots. Throw the carry-on bag on the conveyor belt and grab a plastic bin. Take off the shoes, the belt, the jacket, the cellphone. By the time I was done, I was down to my underwear and wedding ring!

I stood at the radar-screening device ready to walk through, while Rosie was already done, waiting for her bags to come through. On the other side of the screening device, I saw a guy wearing a toy-like sheriff badge going through my suitcase. It seemed a bit unusual, but oh well. He held up a blue, two-foot long machine as high as he could and asked, loudly, "What is this?" He must have thought he had hit the motherlode of banned weapons. This would get him the promotion for sure!

I had been daydreaming a bit, given the "routine," and had even forgotten that Rosie had put the thing in my carry-on in the first place. My mind went totally blank as to what it was called. Without thinking, I said, "It's my wife's vibrator!" Then all hell broke loose.

His eyes became bigger than saucers as he looked for the woman who could own a vibrator so huge! A curious murmur rumbled through the lineup behind me. Rosie screamed, "Hugh!" and with a red face turned back to the guy and said, "No, it's not. It's a *massager.*" The fact that I was in the midst of being frisked made it too late to turn around and catch a different flight to avoid Rosie's wrath. After the expected "I've never been so embarrassed. What were you thinking?" speech, we made our way to the gate and *waited* again. Time passed quickly as we shared a good laugh. That's what I love about Rosie.

For the record, I was right about one thing. She never used it after we got home. Maybe we'll put it in a garage sale as a one-of-a-kind sex toy.

They should create a "Believe It Or Not" section in the World Golf Hall of Fame. When they do, I should get in on the first ballot.

Most golf injuries involve back problems, broken wrists, or permanent migraine headaches from too many three putts. I was leading my flight during a Club Championship. After a couple of celebratory drinks, I was running back to my car in the parking lot when I stepped in a pothole. I fell and chipped a bone in my elbow, broke a bone in my hand, and sprained my wrist *all at the same time.* It had to be some kind of record for multiple injuries in one golf-related mishap.

But the one that will qualify me most for The Hall of Fame is breaking my collarbone.

It was early spring and I was playing in a match play event tournament at Pinebrook, our home club. Match play is when you play against one opponent hole-by-hole, as opposed to counting your total score over eighteen holes.

As always, I carried my clubs with a double strap bag to leave my arms free when walking between shots. It was the sixteenth hole and I was playing my good friend John Maher. I can't remember how the match stood at this point, but it was still "alive," so the hole mattered. After hitting my second shot into the trees, I slung the bag over both shoulders and hiked through the trees, looking for my ball. I kept both hands in my pockets to keep them warm in the cool air. Seeing my ball fifteen feet ahead, I figured I had a good shot at the green. "I'm still in the hole!" I said to myself. Then, I tripped on a tree root. Two hundred pounds of dead weight (I had gained a bit since my teens), plus twenty pounds of golf bag, clubs, and way too many balls, went down like a dead cow at a meat packing plant.

Hands still in my pockets, my collarbone was the first thing to hit the ground. I heard (and felt) it snap like a dry twig. Debris spewed everywhere. Clubs, balls, tees, keys, and coins projected out of the bag when it flipped over my head. When you break a collarbone, you don't need anyone to confirm it. You know. Steve, a friend and fellow player, came up, grabbed my shoulder and said, "Yeah, he's okay." If I could have slugged him, I would have, but the pain was too excruciating!

The guys waved down a Course Marshall to give me a ride back to the clubhouse. It dawned on me that I should have treated the Marshalls better in the past. I could read his mind as he drove up. "Finally, I can get even!" Even the slightest dip caused me a jolt of pain. I swear he swerved to hit *every* pothole.

Meanwhile, back on the green, my opponent John was lining up his putt for par when one of the other guys said, "No need to putt out, John. Hugh's on his way to the hospital in an ambulance. You won!"

I had two choices when I got back to the clubhouse since driving to Emergency was out of the question. Call an ambulance or call Rosie? Despite badly needing a shot of morphine (or a bullet to the head), I rationalized that having Rosie take me to the hospital was the quickest option. We only lived seven minutes away and who knew where the closest ambulance was.

I got on the phone. "Hi Rosie, it's me. I fell and broke my collarbone. Can you run out here and take me to the hospital?" After refusing twice to waste time explaining just <u>how</u> I managed to break a collarbone playing golf, she said, "Okay, I'll come right away."

Now "right away" to most people means *now*! Not to my Rosie. After I waited in the parking lot long enough for five ambulances to have come sequentially, she arrived forty minutes later. I was delirious with pain. "Where the hell have you been?" I screamed.

"Well, I was working outside and had to clean up first." Clean up? She claims she only combed her hair, but I swear she had a shower, manicure, and pedicure! We finally arrived at Emergency, only to find that their sense of urgency was the same as Rosie's—non-existent!

I survived to play another day, but I never carried my bag again. The insurance companies won't allow it. Not too many years later, I would fall while cross-country skiing and break the other collarbone for a matching pair.

I'm not a fan of blind dates, but I suppose they can make sense, most notably when I met Rosie. If both of the "setter-uppers" know the two "set-ups," then they at least know if they're compatible. Such was the case when Rosie and I were set up on the blind date that eventually led to wedded bliss, loosely defined.

Such was not the case when Rosie and I (reluctantly) lined up our friend Joyce Weeks on a blind date. Our good friends Dawn and Glenn Wickerson happened to know a recently divorced friend who they thought could use a social shot in the arm. His name was Drew Glennie. Rosie and I had never met him nor had they met Joyce. This date had about as much chance of success as a mule winning the Kentucky Derby. For the sake of making it less awkward for all, we agreed that the six of us would meet for dinner at a well-known bistro. Surely we could keep the conversation going even if the date was an utter failure.

Like tying my toy guns to my holster, sometimes I overthink the situation instead of just letting it play out. Whatever happens happens, they say!

While driving to the Bistro with Rosie and Joyce, I kept thinking that upon arrival Joyce would not know Drew from Glenn, and Drew would not know Joyce from Rosie—you get the picture. Therefore, I thought it imperative that the introductions be handled properly to minimize confusion and embarrassment. As we entered the restaurant, I saw Glenn and Dawn, and another man who must have been Drew. My mouth got way ahead of my mind and I reached out my hand to Drew. "Hi," I said, "I'm Drew Glennie." He had a startled "So am I" look on his face. I was stunned by what had just come out of my mouth. My error was instantly obvious to everyone. How could I be so stupid?

I sheepishly corrected myself. "Sorry, I'm Hugh. This is

Joyce and that's my wife, Rosie, over there." Thankfully, I got that part right. Everyone had a good laugh and it broke the ice for the rest of the evening. Speaking of ice, the blind date led to a second and last date. The ice never really thawed.

I had returned to Calgary from Palm Desert for a couple of board meetings, so after flying in, I drove my car to my office to check on things before the next morning's meetings. It was late in the evening just before dark as I drove eastbound along Fifth Avenue, a one-way street out of the downtown, to pick up a pizza. One-way avenues in Calgary permit up to four vehicles driving abreast, and that night I had two to my left and one to my right.

Every driver's worst nightmare is hitting a pedestrian. From out of the corner of my eye, I spotted someone starting to run across the intersection in front of us against the light. I guess he thought he could outrun the four of us, all moving in unison and fast, and cross the entire intersection to the other side. His odds of success were the same as a Vegas slot machine coming up four sevens, which is very difficult given there are only three columns on most machines. The pedestrian's gamble gave up only two sevens. He barely made it past the second car before he slammed into the front corner of the third one, mine. I'll never forget the sound of him hitting the side of the car. Indescribable and, fortunately, never duplicated.

I slammed on the brakes and jumped out of my car. The

guy lay in a heap and was not moving. I was sure he was dead. My worst nightmare was happening. I noticed that none of the drivers who had been beside me had stopped. They didn't want to get involved, I guessed. The driver behind me was stopped and waiting, maybe for the light to turn green again. I had a moral dilemma. I was torn between seeing if the guy I hit was alive or making sure the guy behind me stayed put as a witness.

Thankfully, the pedestrian on the ground started to moan and move slightly. I made an executive decision. I chose to run back and tell the driver behind me that I needed him to stay as my only witness. Some might argue my choice was indefensible, but if the guy was to die and I had no witnesses, then I'd be writing these memoirs from prison.

Then, I raced back to help the pedestrian. "Are you okay? Are you okay? Are you okay?" I kept saying. (I didn't know I could repeat something three times in one second.) He wanted to get up, so I helped him to his feet. He was drunk, dirty, and likely homeless. I didn't want him to move until help arrived, remembering my first aid course in Grade Nine: never move the victim. Nothing appeared broken (he wasn't screaming in pain), but he was totally shaken up, maybe even more than I was. He said, "I'm okay. Sorry, sir," and clearly wanted to be on his way. I made him sit down on the sidewalk. Then, I raced back to my car, cars zipping by, and moved it out of the intersection. My side mirror was torn off and there was a big dent on the side. I ran back to the pedestrian and said,

"Wait here, sir. I'm calling the ambulance. It'll be here soon." I had to restrain him from leaving the scene. On my cellphone I called 911 for the first time ever. A soft yet firm female voice answered.

"This is the 911 operator. How might I help you?"

"Yes, I'm calling to report that I've hit a pedestrian trying to cross the street against a light at the corner of Second Street and Fourth Avenue."

She got more details and offered advice while assuring me the ambulance and police would be there shortly. Shortly was an understatement; I could already hear the sirens. Then I looked down the avenue to the west and couldn't believe my eyes. A whole armada was approaching, with four abreast and more coming behind. At least two ambulances and two police cars were racing at full speed, lights flashing and sirens blaring, followed immediately by at least two fire trucks.

Unbelievable! I thought. I only hit one guy. It wasn't a multi-car pileup!

Notwithstanding the colossal waste of taxpayer money with emergency care overkill, I was relieved to see help coming and stepped out to wave them down. They all turned in tandem at the intersection and headed north, completely ignoring my frantic waves and yells of "Over here!" from fifty feet in front of them. At the intersection one block north, they all piled out. At least a dozen policemen, firemen, and emergency personnel ran around looking for an accident that wasn't there.

"Shit." Another dilemma. I couldn't run up there because I had to keep my pedestrian guy from wandering off. I called 911 again.

"Ah, I just called about a pedestrian accident and they all went to the wrong place." She then informed me of a small but important detail. I had given them the wrong intersection. I said fourth and second instead of fifth and second. "Sorry, my mistake!" (This was understandable, given that I had only been at that intersection maybe a thousand times.) Thankfully, the guy was not near death and would survive the delay. Apparently, emergency personnel must ignore idiots like me waving at them and go to the exact location the 911 operator tells them.

From only a block away, I could see a guy answer a phone (my 911 operator, no doubt) and then yell at everyone. Instantly the police, firemen, and emergency guys were all piling into their vehicles and heading one block south towards us, lights flashing and sirens blaring once again. The scene was surreal, like a Keystone Cops silent movie.

In the end, they let the guy go after assuring me he was okay. I guess he must have been "relaxed" when he hit my car. If he'd been sober, I think he would have been badly hurt or even killed.

CHAPTER 28
The Trust

The Trust was one of a half dozen trust model energy companies in Calgary. "Trusts" were the rising "in thing." They consisted of a business model that acquired older producing (less risky) assets from others and managed them more efficiently. All the proceeds would then be paid out each month to shareholders in the form of a largely non-taxable distribution (dividend). But, and this was a key point, trusts always had a "management company" that managed the trust on behalf of the shareholders in return for a fee: fees to produce the properties, fees to sell the properties, and fees to buy new properties. More types of fees were paid to the manager than flying with ten extra bags. But, the shareholders loved their dividends and, as long as they kept flowing, the less they were concerned. The fee structure created a huge conflict of interest for the manager, who was supposed to be looking after shareholder interests.

The CEO, Fred Brown, also owned the management company that operated the trust. Other officers also had ownership in the management company, but Fred had the overwhelming majority share. He was a bright, hard-working, and aggressive entrepreneur, but since management was not his top skillset, he and the Board decided to create a new position of President and COO. The President would provide strategy and day-to-day leadership, including operational execution, and report to the CEO. The Trust also needed to re-establish its credibility in the equity market as it had missed many of its target operating results and, combined with lower oil prices, was now trading at less than half of what it had been at the start.

Throughout my years of executive experience, I learned to pay attention to red flags that pop up when interviewing potential new employees. A red flag could be the littlest thing, such as how they reacted to a certain question, a comment they made about themselves, or just their body language. If I got a feeling of "that doesn't sound good" or "that makes me nervous," I would move on to another candidate. Such was the case with Fred, in reverse. I should have listened to my own advice.

The first red flag popped up while he interviewed me in a small room at a local business club. He lit a cigarette without any consideration for the other person in the room. Inconsiderate. The second red flag popped up after meeting with the vice presidents of the Trust. I met with them after a series of interviews with Fred and one of them asked me, "Why would you want this job? He'll never give up the authority. He's a one-man show."

So why take the job after not one but two red flags? I wish I had a good answer. The best I can come up with is that the opportunity of such a top job clouded my better judgement.

I guess I refused to let such feedback keep me from achieving a higher goal and I thought I could handle the CEO, flaws and all.

The thought of running a medium-sized oil company really appealed to me. I wasn't a geologist, an engineer, or a chartered accountant, but I had touched all the bases. My years at Ashland, Dome, Amoco, and CanWest gave me a well-rounded executive background and good leadership skills, but I also knew that I had a lot to learn about equity markets and running a publicly listed company. No doubt the job would be a big challenge. I may have suffered from the "I made a mistake" mantra in the past, but everything had always worked out in the end. Such would not be the case with The Trust.

My first day did not get off to a good start. When I arrived, a very nice administrative lady greeted me and showed me to my corner office. The office was so big that the desk looked like a lonely island in the middle of a gymnasium. None of the staff came in that morning to welcome me or introduce themselves. It was surreal.

If I had been in the CEO position, I would have been there to show the new president around the company and introduce him to the staff. It would be common courtesy to get things off on the right foot. He never showed his face. It was obvious no one was coming, so I decided that it was time to get started. Down the halls I walked, office by office, introducing myself. I also asked each VP to meet me later to discuss their views and priorities about the company.

I ran into Fred on the second day and suggested we meet to go over some housekeeping items and discuss some priorities. When we met, I suggested that we formalize my authority level. It is critical in such a senior role to know what is expected. I wasn't looking for all the authority, just clarity on what authority I had. This would also be important to the VPs reporting to me. His reply was, "Let's leave it for now and deal with it down the road." He didn't give the slightest indication he intended to delegate anything. I left his office as a president who didn't have the authority to even sign an employee's expense account. This was not good and I knew it. He had no intention of giving up control. All the red flags I had ignored during the interview sessions were now staring me in the face and it was only my first week.

As time went by, things actually proceeded better than I expected. To his credit, he made a better-than-expected effort to let me run with the operations and I was learning a lot about equity markets. Within six months, I had hired a new VP of Operations and oil prices appeared to be rebounding. The Trust started to meet its targets for the first time in years and things were starting to turn around in the equity markets, credibility wise. Investors were telling me that I was making a difference. Fred even made the complimentary comment that he "trusted me and was very happy with what I had done so far."

But a black cloud was billowing on the horizon.

While still at CanWest, I had wanted to enroll in an executive program at a respected university to enhance my management and business skills. The Board was supportive and I was accepted into the six-week program at Stanford University, California, but had not yet attended when the Trust opportunity came along. One of my conditions of acceptance for the position at The Trust was that I be able to attend Stanford. So, six months after starting at The Trust, I headed off for six weeks. Even though I was away, I kept in touch with key people and issues.

My time at Stanford was one of the most satisfying and enlightening experiences of my life. Senior executives from all around the world attended. The professors were top notch. The guest speakers, all Stanford grads, were widely respected people ranging from Condoleezza Rice to George Schultz, a former Secretary of State. I distinctly remember Ms. Rice and how impressed I was with her talk about how the US needed to be less dictatorial in telling other countries how to run their affairs. She then went on to be the next Secretary of State. But nothing changed.

When I returned to The Trust, I could tell on my first day back that things had changed. Fred was *back in the saddle again,* having re-established old relationships during my absence. He was back to being the entrepreneur and sole decision maker, and relishing it. Whether it was planned or unplanned, it didn't really matter. It was clear that our relationship had changed and, as a consequence, my relationship with the VPs had changed.

The relationship between a CEO and COO is a real

challenge in the best of circumstances, but it's compounded when the CEO is an entrepreneur who's used to being the sole authority. The company was his baby. I know of several former COOs in the business who exited because of the exact issue I had at The Trust. Some say these types of jobs are "Mission Impossible."

Somehow, we all managed to make it work over the next several months and continued to post improved results. The doubling of the share price reflected this.

The beginning of the end was what I saw as a conflict of interest situation between what I thought was right and what he thought was right. To be clear, what he had asked me to do was not illegal, but by any definition it was aggressive. Successful enterpreneurs often aggressively push the boundaries of conflict in their favor, but to me it was a matter of principle. I drew a line in the sand. A friend once advised me to "only draw a line in the sand on a windy day. In case you change your mind!" It wasn't a windy day, so there was no going back.

When the CEO and COO clash, someone is going to lose and it's usually the COO. Three months later, after just two years on the job, Fred called me down and fired me. It was still a shock. After thirty years without a hiccup, my career was, for all intents and purposes, over. His reason: "He didn't trust me anymore." If "trust" meant turning a blind eye to the conflictsof interest I percieved as real, he was right. A couple of directors met with me privately over lunch and said that it all had nothing to do with my performance and everything to do with the personality conflict. They couldn't fire the management company, so there was no other choice. I didn't believe them then and still don't. They had options.

It was a tough job to fill and, without question, I was not the next Jack Welch (former CEO of GE). Could I have done better? Absolutely. The Trust had had very poor quality assets when I arrived and part of my strategy was to squeeze more value out of them. After regaining our credibility, more and quicker value would have occurred had we done a large acquisition to marginalize the existing poor properties.

Could I have handled the conflict of interest issue better? Maybe, but you are who you are and I was proud of what we had achieved and that I had taken a stance on principle. The organization had been strengthened, market credibility restored, and the share price had doubled from when I started. More than one of my executive team volunteered to me afterwards that I was in a no-win situation right from the start. Not paying attention to the red flags before I accepted the job meant I had no one to blame but myself.

Whatever happened to that infamous issue that ultimately drove the final wedge between us? Well, it never came to pass, but the damage was done. Over time, the share price rose before falling back down once again. Ultimately, the Trust was sold.

I have often asked myself whether I did the right thing, given how it so adversly affected my career. The answer is always the same: yes. Someone once said, "takers eat well, but givers sleep well." Amen to that.

CHAPTER 29
Phoenix

Companies that fail and then rise from the ashes have been dubbed Phoenixes. Thousands of executives have experienced what I have. In some cases, it's their own doing. But the why doesn't really matter because people draw their own conclusions anyway, right or wrong. After a short period of mourning and feeling like the world was coming to an end (and that's exactly what it's like after being fired), it was my turn to try and rise from the ashes.

After being fired, I got nothing but positive feedback from people in the business, the real movers and shakers. Comments like "You have a great reputation" or "We know where the real problem was" were all appreciated. Even shareholders and other Trust CEOs called to show support, which I found very gratifying. Despite all the reassurances, my executive career was stalled. Once you've been tainted, rightly or wrongly, you become a pariah. Intuition told me that the Second Coming would occur before my next CEO position.

The next couple of years weren't totally without action. In conjunction with an investment banking firm, I researched and authored a major study on energy trusts from an "independent" perspective. They sold it to many of their clients (mutual funds who invested in trusts) and even to a few trusts. A friend who was highly respected in the business, told me that my report was the "best report ever written on trusts." Given my observation and experience, I emphasized the inherent conflict of interest between the management company and the shareholders because of the fee structure. Not surprisingly the trust managers in town didn't exactly welcome the report. Eventually, the structure of the trusts changed to eliminate the conflict of interest. I don't take full credit for it, but I believe that my trust report was the catalyst for the major institutional shareholders to insist on change.

On another front, I met a gentleman who I had coincidentally graduated from university with some thirty years earlier. He was "in between jobs" as well and we hit it off immediately. We joined forces and bid on an oil well service company that was for sale. Our bid came up short, but we had no regrets trying. You have to kick a lot of tires before you find the right car.

Being in the right place at the right time could not have been truer than one night when I stood in line at McDonald's. A fellow at the front turned around with his order and was heading back out when he saw me and said hello. It was Mike Doyle, who had worked for Dome Petroleum in the Geophysical Department. We never worked together, but knew each other well enough to take time for a quick catch-up visit. He asked what I was up to, which was easy to answer. "Very little," I said, "but looking for opportunities." We exchanged business cards and he was off and out the door.

Within a couple of days, my phone rang. It was Mike, wondering if I wanted to pop over to his office and chat about something. I met Mike, Neil Taylor (who had once worked for me at Dome), Barry Wright, Carter Siebens, and some other gentlemen I hadn't met before. (Coincidentally, Carter's father owned Siebens Oil and Gas, the company Dome acquired that kick-started my career).

"We're thinking of starting up a small oil company," they said and from there we discussed a concept they had come up with. Over the next couple of weeks, our conversations culminated in the formation of a new junior oil company. I became President and CEO and Barry and others became directors.

Sam the Record Man was a famous music store in Toronto. It had formed a public company called Samstown to sell CDs over the Internet, leading edge at the time. A great concept, but like many things in business, timing is everything. They no sooner got it started than the industry took a 180-degree turn. A new thing called "downloading" music for free had come along. Their business plan lasted as long as it took someone to log onto a computer and download the music for nothing. It went bust, leaving a publicly listed shell of a company with a bunch of tax losses. With an infusion of cash, Samstown became Kelso Energy Ltd. I named it Kelso after the champion racehorse of the 1950s—a proven winner!

Our first priority was building a team of technical

professionals and then, hopefully, raise enough equity to acquire lands, drill wells, get production, go to the bank, and live happily ever after. I hired an experienced geologist and a reservoir engineer to form the three-man nucleus of Kelso and then set about trying to raise capital, which is a tough hurdle. Many new companies are not able to do so. Capital markets are fickle, coming and going very quickly with oil and gas prices or management team's failures and successes. I'll never forget the first call I got from Acumen Capital, our investment banker, when the equity issue was underway. I was nervously waiting to see if anyone would have enough faith in my new team and me to invest money.

"Hugh, your reputation is even better than we had imagined. A lot of people believe in you and the issue is already oversubscribed. You need to consider raising the maximum limit," he said. I told him I'd get back to him. I couldn't stop smiling. The Phoenix had risen and we were on our way. There is life after death after all.

We raised $6 million, which is small compared to today's IPOs, but back then, considering our lack of track record, it was a very good start. Among the hundreds of investors were family and friends who assumed I'd do well. Everyone got into the action: my mother and siblings and their neighbours and friends, and in turn their neighbours and friends. They ignored the risk of investing in the oil and gas business and figured my company was as safe as a bond! A scary thought. There's a famous story about Joseph Kennedy, JFK's billionaire father, who sold all his stocks in 1929 just ahead of the big crash. He decided to sell everything the day his shoeshine boy gave him a surefire stock tip. That kid's great grandson probably bought Kelso. I really appreciated everybody's faith in me, but it did turn up the pressure to perform.

I never could have imagined as a little boy seeing my first drilling rig near our ranch, that I would return some forty years later to drill a well. But that's exactly what happened. Our first well was located only fifteen miles northeast of our old ranch back at Throne. It was a successful oil well, and Kelso was off to a good start. The second and third wells we drilled were okay, but not nearly as good as the first one. It seemed we had drilled the best prospect first. Drilling is a tough business and did I mention risky?

Over the next two years, we acquired various different parcels of drilling rights in Alberta and British Columbia, raised some additional capital, and drilled a successful gas well. In this business you need not just good skills but also good luck. There are dozens of entrepreneurs who, despite best efforts, came up short starting an oil company. Others may hit it big the first time, then fail miserably the second time, or if not then, the third. In my view, lots of guys who succeed the first time never give enough credit to luck. Luck is a huge part of the business. I highly respect those who have been successful more than once.

We had some good luck initially, but soon had a bad run. One big problem, which I took full responsibility for, was that our plays became too spread out. Kelso was not as focused as it should have been. My technical team was what I call risk-dysfunctional, which compounded the problem. Both the VP Exploration and VP Production were fine people and very good technically, but at the opposite ends of the scale when it came to risk. The VP Exploration's vocabulary did not contain the word "risk." The VP Production was the polar opposite. He was totally risk adverse. This, of course, left me to make the final call. Some of my calls turned out well and some not so well.

After three years, we had some production and some cash in the bank, but I knew we had missed our opportunity with investors to "put up the numbers." As they say in the business, you can only go back to the well so often. More importantly, I didn't want to risk spending the last dollar and the shareholders getting nothing. It was also very important to me that we pay off the debenture to the original backers of Kelso. We could have hung on for years paying ourselves salaries, but I wanted to do what was best for shareholders. Some months later, I recommended to the Board that we do a merger with another company of similar size with a different technical team. This was completed in 2006. Kelso was no more.

I could spend days second-guessing decisions or missed opportunities. The merger turned out to be an utter disaster. One of the attractions of the deal was the other company had a large investor who had made a lot of money in other ventures and sat on their Board of Directors. I convinced myself that he had connections to large pools of equity capital, which would be critical for Kelso going forward. In time, I saw him as a promoter whose primary goal was to flip (sell) the company as opposed to being a long-term growth investor. Unbeknownst to me and two other directors, the new management team was encouraged to drill high-risk wells hoping for a home run. Spending our limited cash on two expensive dry holes made the new company unsalvageable. Two of us resigned from the Board and the company, for all intents and purposes, was no more. Family and friends who had invested purely on faith in me lost much of their money. Fortunately, all were wise enough not to invest their entire net worth or children's inheritance, so they accepted the outcome as a risk of investing and moved on.

You do your best and hope for the best. Such is the nature of the oil business. I know I was naïve to think that the merger had much chance of success given the players involved. A far better decision would have been to change the technical team, preserve the cash, and completely change our business strategy. I had invested a lot of my own money in Kelso and should not have done the merger. Once the toothpaste is out of the tube, you can't put it back in. I wish I could, but so do a lot of entrepreneurs who start companies and experience failure before success. My age was now becoming a factor. In my late fifties, I didn't have time to start over. Hello retirement.

After leaving The Trust, I was pleased to be approached to join a number of Boards of Directors. They ranged from a junior oil and gas company, a large service company, a wind power company, an investment banking firm, and an oil and gas trust. The oil and gas trust, Crescent Point Energy, has since grown to be a Top 100 company in Canada with a market capitalization of over $14 billion, thanks to a tremendously talented executive team and staff.

Being on Boards sounds glamorous, but in fact carries huge responsibilities and potential personal liabilities. And they don't all succeed, most often through no fault of the Board. I use these opportunities to stay intellectually challenged and contribute to a company's success, all the while gradually transitioning into retirement. I call it semi-retirement.

Reflecting on my career is like looking through a kaleidoscope. No two opportunities or outcomes were the same. Some turned out fantastic while others not so good. If ascending to the highest mountaintop is a measure of career success, then I guess I came up a bit short. But, for me, a better measure is whether one does his best with what he is given. There were things that went right and things that went not-so-right, decisions taken and choices made, but I have few regrets. I never would have thought, sitting in my car after the devastating Texaco interview forty years earlier, that my career would be so fruitful and positive. I may have started the race several yards behind the starting line, but after a lot of laps, I made it to the finish line, and in respectable time.

I consider myself truly lucky. Throughout my career I encountered people ranging from discriminatory to supportive and from selfish to loyal, but the vast majority were good and decent people, all trying to do their best. I cannot say enough thanks to all of those whose paths I crossed along the way.

CHAPTER 30
The Love of my Life

After our blind date, Rosie and I dated semi-seriously in between her understandably higher priorities of her daughters, Tracey and Heather. She was a devoted mom who drove the girls to soccer, gymnastics, school events, and the Young Canadians, a song and dance group for the Calgary Stampede stage show.

Our first Christmas and New Year's "as an item" was unique and unforgettable. Rosie had decided to go home to Fredericton to spend the holiday season with her parents and siblings since it was the kids' turn to spend the holidays with their dad. Over a nice dinner out before she left, we discussed all the usual topics from what we were both doing, what the kids were doing, how our respective jobs were going, and what I hoped the two of us would be doing later that night. The conversation eventually turned to smoking. I still smoked, despite indicating, placating mostly, that I would quit someday. How I let my guard down so easily still baffles me, but somehow I managed to state that I planned to quit smoking as a New Year's resolution. I'm sure I'm the only person to have had such a New Year's resolution!

"This time I mean it," I said, foolishly ignoring my lack

of success with the previous five years of resolutions to do the same thing.

"You promise?" Rosie shot back before I had any chance of withdrawing the comment.

"Yes." No short answer would match the importance of this one, other than "I do."

That year, I was hosting a New Year's Eve party at my condo. From the time Rosie had gotten on the plane and left town, I never thought seriously of quitting smoking or the promise I had made. Same old same old! Maybe next year! I had completely put it out of my mind.

At exactly five minutes to midnight, measured by the most accurate atomic clock, the phone rang. Despite the noise and everyone screaming in the background, I managed to hear it. "Who the hell would be phoning here now?" I wondered. With a half burned cigarette between my fingers, I grabbed the phone.

"Hello!" I yelled, thinking, as always, that the other person couldn't hear either.

"Hi, it's me!" It was Rosie.

"Oh, hi!" I said, genuinely pleased that she had called me from so far away. I was proud to think that maybe she really did like me.

"Did you quit smoking?"

She had remembered! This was an intervention without

the psychiatrist. I looked at the cigarette in my hand. The truth was I had not quit. I was waving the smoke away as we talked. Fortunately, Skype did not exist.

"Yes," I replied.

She responded ecstatically at the other end.

As I hung up the phone, I knew I had to honour what I had said. I butted out the cigarette in a nearby ashtray. Twenty-nine years later I have never lit up another cigarette. It was extremely difficult those first few months, but I made it through. About four months into self-counselled rehab, I recall driving home from work and realizing that the entire day had gone by and I had not thought about lighting up. It was only then that I knew I could do it. Rosie's stubbornness about my smoking made me a better and healthier person and maybe I'm still here because of it. I give her full credit.

As the months went by, our relationship grew. That little speck of commitment on the far horizon, at first hardly visible with the naked eye, grew in size and proximity. We were heading towards a monumental decision that would bind us together forever or end it.

Ironically, it was the oil business that brought Rosie to Calgary and ultimately meeting me. After one year of university, she married an engineering student and they had a daughter, Tracey. He got a job with a large oil company, so the three of them packed up and moved to Drayton Valley, Alberta. Rosie holds no fond memories of Drayton Valley, other than the birth of her second daughter, Heather. It was still a new, growing, and tough oil town situated in the bush and quite a shock for someone from 200-year-old staid Fredericton. They survived Drayton better than their marriage. In a few years, she was on her own raising two young daughters in the city of Calgary. I don't know how it all transpired to that point, nor do I much care. In her words, it was the "before Hugh" era. What I saw and admired was a woman who was totally focused on raising her two girls and sacrificing whatever was necessary to do so.

Rosie was a true blue Maritime girl, all about the water, fishing, and fall colours. She was right brain dominant—a wonderful artist, creative, soft, and all about family. I was a prairie boy, all about oil, grassland, and cattle. I was all left brain—classic Type A, hyperactive, all business, and chasing the pot at the end of the rainbow. As it turned out, Rosie was my rainbow.

She was thirty-seven and a single mother with two kids. At thirty-five, I was single, answerable to no one, and had a promising career. I was living the good life of dating, trips with my buddies, and no accountability. She knew what marriage entailed, good and bad, having been there and done that. For every ounce of marriage experience she had, I had a pound of naivety and inexperience. Everything I knew about marriage came from watching "Father Knows Best."

If opposites truly attract, then we were as solid as the north and south ends of a very short magnet. So, with nothing in common, the obvious thing to do was . . . get married!

Her daughters Heather, then twelve, and Tracey, then seventeen, had a rather different take on us getting married, almost bordering on hostile. Typical of teenagers, they had their views and opinions and saw no barriers to making sure I knew where they stood. If I thought this new family would be sitting around the fireplace holding hands and singing "Kumbaya," I had to think again. They had never really understood or accepted why their parents got divorced in the first place and my presence was interpreted as eliminating any chance of reconciliation. In their minds, their mother marrying someone else was the worst possible outcome.

The date we chose, June 9, turned out to be a mistake, and we both should have known better. Early June may be a good traditional time to get married, but it was too close to Tracey's Grade Twelve graduation date. Tracey was proud of her accomplishment, as she should have been and there we were stealing her moment in the sun. A good friend of Rosie's, who had known Tracey all her life, pointed this out to us many years later. We had created an unnecessary anxiety that only made matters worse.

But, there was no turning back. The wedding was a go!

I had three good friends stand up with me at the

wedding: Mike, Oz, and Phil. Rosie wanted her daughters to be there, too. I understood, but argued that maybe Heather was too young. It would be uncomfortable and not the most pleasant experience for Ozzie to pair up with a child at the wedding, and particularly at the banquet. I lost the argument (the beginning of the norm!), but the girls put on positive faces and were a true delight, especially when the two of them sang "Some Enchanted Evening" at the church ceremony. Ozzie persevered like a true friend and did a great job of making small talk with Heather during the banquet and first dance.

I suppose every groom feels the same way when he first sees his wife-to-be walk down the aisle towards the altar. Wow! Rosie was absolutely radiant with her huge smile—the same smile that had captivated me when I met her at her door on our blind date.

During our vows, another unforgettable moment occurred when my anxiousness got the best of me.

"And will you, Hugh…" the minister started.

"I will," I said, interrupting.

"Take Rosemary…" the minister continued.

"I will," I said again.

The minister leaned over and quietly whispered, "I'll tell you when to say 'I will.'"

The wedding guests roared in unison.

Then came the all-important question, where I held my

breath. "Does anyone here object to this union or forever hold your peace?" Thankfully, Rosie's girls took a pass.

Ever since, if I get too anxious, we have a laugh and say, "I will, I will, I will."

This year marks our twenty-ninth year of, dare I say it, wedded bliss. I have often joked that to get married, I gave up sex, smoking, and half my money! Well, maybe only partially true, but it's been worth it.

We certainly had our challenges early on. I had been single for a long time, so getting married and inheriting two teenage girls at the same time was a shock to my system. For quite some time, I thought it was too much change at once. Rosie felt pretty much the same. She was used to being the *only* authority in the house and the difficulties of melding a new person into the family seemed to catch her off guard. She felt torn between her kids and her new husband. She never said it, but I think she too initially thought getting married was a mistake. Had we had done a poll of the kids' opinions, they would have checked off the "End It!" box. Nowadays, divorce is the easy way out. Back then, you tried harder to make it work and, besides, we both had too much pride to not hang in there.

Once we moved to a new and more spacious home, things started to settle down. After Heather moved out (we hoped she wouldn't, but such is the choice of a child who has two sets of parents) and Tracey was gone to University of British Columbia, it gave the two of us time and space to build our own relationship. The song "Wind Beneath My Wings" is an accurate account of the support I had from Rosie in my career. I am very fortunate to have had a successful career, but I would not have made it without Rosie.

Over the years we've been married, I've learned a lot from Rosie. I've often mentioned to her that I'm not sure I'd have gotten by without her sage and unsolicited advice. Her advice to me reflects the degree of perfection she has.

If the parking lot at the mall has 140 empty spots, there's only one right one—and never the one I pick. When parking the car, it must be dead centre between the lines. Measured! After forty years of driving to work downtown, I still don't know the best route when we go out for dinner. If the car has less than three quarters of a tank of gas, it's empty. "I'm not walking if we run out of gas!" she reminds me.

When the airlines suggest arriving ninety minutes prior to departure because of security lineups, they really mean three hours. When we casually discuss a trip idea two years hence, she says I need to be more decisive and commit to the places and dates. Like the one she just found on the Internet in the middle of the same night we first discussed it. "They're going to disappear any moment," she'll say. She thinks it's perfectly normal to have a photo of us eating at every restaurant we've ever been to. She answers questions put to me better than I can! In her mind, portfolio investing is a failure if there's even a single losing investment. By last count, I owe her $5,000 in Scrabble losses. All of this drives me crazy, but it's what I love about her.

And the real bonus was the relationship that grew between Tracey, Heather, and me. From a beginning that almost ended before it started, our relationship has grown stronger each year. I don't share their DNA, but in every other aspect I try to be there for them and their families. More than once, I've told Rosie that the greatest gift she ever gave me was an extended family of my own, including five perfect grandchildren. I call them my "do-dads," which is what Dad called us when we were little. Tracey and Nick have Alexander, Sophie, and Sterling, while Heather and Kai have little Islie and Madeline. The grandchildren love Pop for who he is, no questions asked. I never imagined any of this fifty years ago while alone at that drive-in on New Year's Eve. Like the line from the movie *Forrest Gump,* "Life is like a box of chocolates. You never know what you're gonna get." I chose well.

One of my favourite songs is Neil Diamond's "I Am I Said." The lyrics reflect exactly what Rosie means to me and the difference she's made in my life: "Have you ever heard of the frog, who dreamed of being a king and then became one? Well, except for the names and a few other changes, if you talk about me . . . the story's the same one . . ."

Rosie is not just my wife, but my live-in speech therapist,

grammar teacher, and translator. Even with a university education, I developed bad grammar habits that she promptly corrected until I got them right every time. She drove me crazy about grammar, but I'm glad she did. Countless times I ask her how to properly pronounce a word. Often, but not always, it's a simple case of me not hearing it properly. Then, with her help, voila! I get it right. It was so easy. Unfortunately, the little curveball nature threw at me will always make it impossible to say some words perfectly, but I'm okay with that. On more than one occasion over the years, Rosie has told the waiter what I ordered or grabbed the phone and clarified what I was trying to communicate.

Today, in our retirement, we own a second home in California at a community called The Lakes. We named our place Rusty Spurs, a place where old cowboys go to retire. The Lakes was a great choice by all standards, except one—I cannot pronounce it properly. When the local people ask me where I live, they no more know after I tell them than before. Often I simply say, "At the corner of Cook Street and Country Club Drive." I can see their minds churning with "What housing development is near there? Oh, The Lakes!"

Just the other night at our boys' weekly poker game, I used the term "counterfeited," which is a common term in Omaha or Texas Hold'em. A couple of the players looked at me funny and said, "What did you say?" Then, they looked at each other and said, "Did he say powdered sugar? I thought he said powdered sugar."

What Did You Say?

Recently, I went to a local diner to have some breakfast. I sat at the counter and ordered bacon and eggs. Noticing that I had no fork or knife, I asked the waiter, "And may I have utensils, please?" A minute later, he brought me a "pencil." Even though I was by myself, I laughed out loud.

Some things just never change!

CHAPTER 31
Words of Wisdom

Recently, Rosie and I took Alexander, Sophie, and Sterling to an ice cream shop (ever the spoilers) and, while sitting and eating my cone, I looked at a handwritten message on a blackboard. It read: "Dream big, work hard, stay focused, and surround yourself with good people." My philosophy exactly. I don't know if it was original or not (probably not), but this little ice cream shop message said it all, and better than I could have ever have expressed it.

One day our grandchildren might read these memoirs. I can only hope that before drifting off to sleep from complete boredom, they take away something of value.

Based on my own experiences, here are some "nevers":

1. *Never shop for earmuffs without money.*
2. *Never trust a dog after dark.*
3. *Never board a small plane after having a few.*
4. *Never confuse Hu with Who.*
5. *Never stop laughing at yourself.*
6. *Never compromise on ethics.*
7. *Never quit trying.*

And, just for good measure, here are some "dos":

1. *If you see a red flag—pay attention! It's red for a reason.*
2. *Be a win-win in business. When everyone wins, you do too.*
3. *Take risks. They may not all work out, but you'll regret not trying.*
4. *Give others a second chance.*
5. *Work hard.*
6. *Do your best.*
7. *Name your children something simple to say and spell.*
8. *Raise your children on a farm.*
9. *Laugh at yourself.*
10. *Be generous.*

CHAPTER 32
Signing Off

My life has been no more special than anyone else's and certainly I'm not famous, so why did I write this book? I wrote this collection of memories for a whole host of reasons.

For one, I wish that my grandparents had put down in writing some of their life experiences for future generations to share. Every generation seems to believe that their life and times aren't important and future generations won't care. Someday, my grandchildren may like to know more about their "Pop" and the times he lived in and how he and Nana came to know each other. And maybe someday I'll write the sequel about Rosie and our years together, our great family, and all the wonderful friends we made along the way.

Second, someone encouraged me to write my memoirs—Bruna Martinuzzi, my former Human Resources Manager at CanWest. We've kept in touch over the years and she is now a successful management training book writer and speaker in her own right. It was her persistent encouragement that I write about my life experiences to help young cleft-afflicted people that really convinced me to put something on paper.

"The world needs a book like yours. There's a need out there," she would say. "You can go on *Oprah*." Well, Bruna, it turned out to be just a collection of memories and I'll have to settle for being a guest at one of my do-dads' show-and-tells, but maybe, with the help of a *real* writer, there's a short motivational book or blog posting buried in here somewhere.

To me, the whole exercise was simply a chance to reflect on the past before age catches up to me. Putting pen to paper though proved more difficult than I thought. I am not a creative person in the slightest. Recalling the past—the funny and heartbreaking, the good and not-so-good, the successes and failures—was good for my soul. I was incredibly lucky to have the support of my wife, family, friends, mentors, and associates. I took the road less travelled, but with these people in my life, it was much smoother.